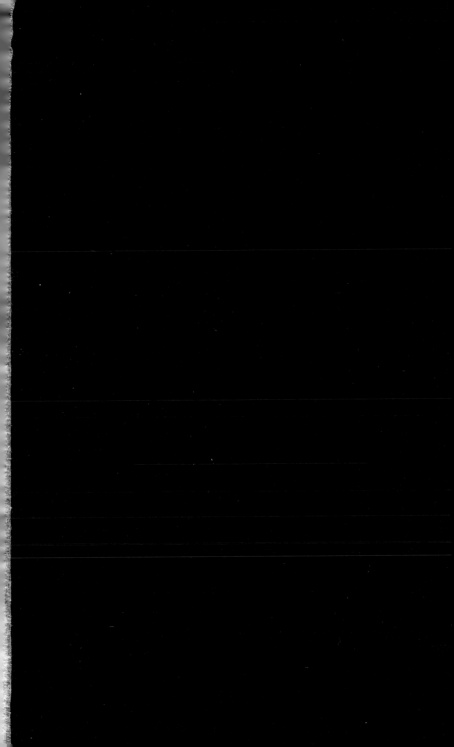

REAL ESTATE

By the same author

Ophelia and the Great Idea

Beautiful Mutants

Swallowing Geography

The Unloved

Diary of a Steak

Billy & Girl

Pillow Talk in Europe and Other Places

Swimming Home

Black Vodka

Things I Don't Want to Know

Hot Milk

The Cost of Living

The Man Who Saw Everything

REAL ESTATE

Deborah Levy

HAMISH HAMILTON
an imprint of
PENGUIN BOOKS

HAMISH HAMILTON

UK | USA | Canada | Ireland | Australia
India | New Zealand | South Africa

Hamish Hamilton is part of the Penguin Random House group of companies
whose addresses can be found at global.penguinrandomhouse.com.

Penguin
Random House
UK

First published 2021
001

Set in 14.2/18.7 pt Fournier MT Std
Typeset by Jouve (UK), Milton Keynes
Printed and bound in Great Britain by Clays Ltd, Elcograf S.p.A.

The authorized representative in the EEA is Penguin Random House Ireland,
Morrison Chambers, 32 Nassau Street, Dublin D02 YH68

A CIP catalogue record for this book is available from the British Library

ISBN: 978–0–241–26801–8

www.greenpenguin.co.uk

FSC
www.fsc.org
MIX
Paper from
responsible sources
FSC® C018179

Penguin Random House is committed to a sustainable future for our business, our readers and our planet. This book is made from Forest Stewardship Council® certified paper.

I'm in front of this feminine landscape
Like a branch in the fire.

Paul Éluard, 'Ecstasy'
Translated by Peter Read

I

LONDON

In the winter of January 2018, I bought a small banana tree from a flower stall outside Shoreditch High Street station. It seduced me with its shivering, wide green leaves, also with the new leaves that were furled up, waiting to stretch out into the world. The woman who sold it to me had long fake eyelashes, blue-black and luscious. In my mind's eye her lashes stretched all the way from the bagel shops and grey cobblestones of East London to the deserts and mountains of New Mexico. The delicate winter blooms at her stall had me thinking about the artist Georgia O'Keeffe and the way she painted flowers. It was as if she were introducing each one of them to us for the first time. In O'Keeffe's hands they became peculiar, sexual, uncanny. Sometimes her flowers looked as if they had stopped breathing under the scrutiny of her gaze.

> When you take a flower in your hand and really look at it, it's your world for the moment. I want to give that world to someone else.
>
> Georgia O'Keeffe, quoted in the *New York Post*, 16 May 1946

She had found her final house in New Mexico, a place to live and work at her own pace. As she insisted, it was something she had to have. She had spent years restoring this low-slung adobe house in the desert before she finally moved into it. A while back, when I made the journey to Santa Fe, New Mexico, partly to see O'Keeffe's house, I remember feeling dizzy when I arrived at Albuquerque airport. My driver told me it was because we were 6,000 feet above sea level. The dining room in my hotel, owned by a Native American family, had a tall adobe fireplace built into the wall in the shape of an ostrich egg. I had never seen an oval fireplace before. It was October and it was snowing, so I pulled up a chair in front of the glowing logs and sipped a cup of smoky clear mescal, which was apparently good for above-sea-level sickness. The curved fireplace made me feel welcome and calm. It pulled me into its centre. Yes, I loved this burning egg. That fireplace *was something I had to have.*

I was also searching for a house in which I could live and work and make a world at my own pace, but even in my imagination this home was blurred, undefined, not real, or not realistic, or lacked realism. I yearned for a grand old house (I had now added an oval fireplace to its architecture) and a pomegranate tree in the garden. It had fountains and wells, remarkable circular stairways, mosaic floors, traces of the rituals of all who had lived there before me. That is to say the house was lively, it had enjoyed a life. It was a loving house.

The wish for this home was intense, yet I could not place it geographically, nor did I know how to achieve such a spectacular house with my precarious income. All the same, I added it to my imagined property portfolio, along with a few other imagined minor properties. The house with the pomegranate tree was my major acquisition. In this sense, I owned some unreal estate. The odd thing was that every time I tried to see myself inside this grand old house, I felt sad. It was as if the search for home was the point, and now that I had acquired it and the chase was over, there were no more branches to put in the fire.

In the meanwhile I had to get my new banana tree home from Shoreditch on a bus and a train to my crumbling apartment block on the hill. It was growing in a pot, about one foot high. The flower seller with long, luscious fake eyelashes told me she reckoned it wanted to live a more humid life. It had been a cold winter in the UK so far and we agreed we were also yearning for a more humid life.

While I was on the train to Highbury and Islington, I added a few more details to my unreal estate. Despite the egg-shaped fireplace my major house was obviously situated in a hot climate, near a lake or the sea. A life without swimming every day was not a life I wanted. It was hard to admit this to myself, but the ocean and the lake were more important to me than the house. In fact I would be content to live in a humble wooden cabin on the edge of an ocean or a lake, but somehow I looked down on myself for not having a bigger dream.

It seemed that acquiring a house was not the same thing as acquiring a home. And connected to home was a question I swatted away every time it landed too near me. Who else was living with me in the grand old house with the pomegranate tree? Was I alone with the melancholy fountain for company? No. There was definitely someone else there with me, perhaps even cooling their feet in that fountain. Who was this person?

A phantom.

My plan for the banana tree was to add it to the garden I had made on three shelves in my bathroom. I knew from the succulents enjoying their displaced life in North London that it would like the warm steam from the shower. My apartment block had still not been restored, seven years after I moved into it, and the grey communal corridors were in an even worse state of disrepair. Like love, they badly needed restoring. The banana plant didn't care about the state of the building. If anything, it seemed ecstatic to move in and began to show off, unfurling its wide, veined leaves.

My daughters became curious about the attention I was bestowing upon this plant. They both agreed that I was obsessed with the banana tree because my youngest daughter was going to be leaving home for university soon. That tree, my youngest (age eighteen) told me, was my *third child*. Its job was to replace her when she left home. In the months of its growing, she would ask, 'How is your new child doing?' and she would point to the tree.

I would soon be living alone. If I had made another sort of life since I separated from her father, it seemed that soon, age fifty-nine, I would be required to make another life all over again. I did not want to think about this, so I began to pack up a few things to take to my new writing shed.

2

It was literally an oasis built amongst palms, ferns and tall bamboo. I couldn't believe my eyes or my luck. The garden surrounding my new writing shed, which was built on decking, resembled a tropical rainforest. Really, I should have gifted my banana tree to this garden, but as my daughters had suggested, it had become part of the family. My shed landlord gave me the key to the garden side entrance so I did not need to interrupt him in the main house. The day I arrived he placed a hyacinth inside the shed. Its perfume was overwhelming and welcoming in equal measure. Perhaps its perfume was even violent. I unpacked three Russian glasses with silver handles for coffee, a cafetière, one jar of coffee (100% Arabica), two tangerines, a bottle of ruby port from Porto (left over from Christmas), two bottles of sparkling water, almond biscuits from Italy, three teaspoons, my laptop and two books. And an adaptor of course, this time a coil with four sockets. My shed landlord, who was born in New Zealand, had planted the garden around my new shed with flair, imagination, maybe even nostalgia. I thought he had created something of New Zealand in London NW8, that is to say, his homeland was haunting this London garden because it still haunted him.

At a literary festival in Austria, I had met a writer from Romania who arrived in Switzerland as a refugee in 1987. She had rented a room in a Zurich street which she thought resembled her street in Bucharest. And then she had made her Zurich room look similar to her room in Bucharest. She reminded me that when I was twenty-nine, I had written a book of linked stories called *Swallowing Geography*. Actually, I hadn't forgotten that I had written a whole book, but I was pleased it felt new to her. She told me that she had pinned to the wall by her bed the words of the female narrator:

> Each new journey is a mourning for what has been left behind. The wanderer sometimes tries to recreate what has been left behind, in a new place.

It seemed that I was now busy making the new writing shed look quite similar to my old writing shed.

I uncoiled the lead for the sockets and made a pot of coffee. And then I raised my glass of coffee to that writer from Bucharest. 'How are you?' I said to her in my head. 'I hope things are going well for you.' We had laughed together in Austria because she told me that someone in the audience had put up their hand and declared they wanted to know more about the country of her birth. She had lived in one of the most oppressive communist regimes in the world and was waiting for a big question about how a writer might work with language when freedoms are demolished, or about the struggle to remember and forget and put herself together again. She feared she might not be able to answer it. 'Could you please tell me if it's safe to drink the tap water there?' this person wanted to know. To which she and I had later both added, 'Could you please give me the Wi-Fi password, and are there mosquitoes?'

This writing shed was very close to the life I wanted, even if it was a temporary arrangement. I mean it was not my real estate, I did not own it, I was renting it, but I owned its mood. Even the English birds chirping and calling in NW8 seemed tropical. I had still not completely moved out of my old writing shed, but Celia (my old shed landlady) had put her house up for sale and I knew I had to make other arrangements.

The new shed was near the Abbey Road, where I would set my novel *The Man Who Saw Everything*. I was haunting the Abbey Road and it was haunting me. 'Home is where the haunt is,' wrote the late, great essayist Mark Fisher, and that was certainly true for me. In a way I was still a spectral occupant of the old writing shed because many of my books were languishing on its shelves. My desktop computer still lived on the desk, now covered in a white sheet. The Provençal heater I had bought to heat it in winter had become a home for small spiders and their vast geometric webs.

Meanwhile, a spectre lurked right here in the new shed on the first page of one of the books I had brought with me. I noticed there was an inscription inside it from the father of my children in the year 1999, when I was married and lived in our family house.

To my Darling love for last Christmas of the Century with 1000 years of devotion

It was a shock. I had to put the book down and let the hyacinth's perfume numb this moment like morphine. Then I picked the book up again and gazed at the inscription. I wondered who that spectral woman was, twenty years ago, the woman who had received this book with its loving inscription.

I tried to connect with Her (who is my younger self), to remember how she had responded to this gift at the time. I did not want to see her too clearly. But I did try to wave to her. I knew she would not want to see me (*so there you are, nearly sixty and alone*) and I did not want to see her either (*so there you are, forty years old, hiding your talent, trying to keep your family together*), but she and I haunted each other across time.

Hello. Hello. Hello.

My younger self (fierce, sad) knew that I did not judge her. We had both lost and gained various things in the twenty years that separated us from the moment of my receiving this gift with its loving inscription. Now and again I got flashbacks to the family house. It was haunted by my unhappiness, and though I tried to change the mood and find something good about it, the house would not oblige my wish to make a new memory of the mood. The crumbling apartment block on the hill was much more modest than that house, yet its mood was upbeat, serene, gentler, hopeful rather than hopeless.

*

I glanced at the inscription again.

To my Darling love for last Christmas of the Century

The odd thing was that the book itself (by a famous male author) was about a man who has left his family and sets about making a new life with various women. One of these young women adores him so much that she reaches over to take the snot out of his nostrils. She has made him her purpose in life and we are clueless about her own sense of purpose. They have lots of sex but we have no idea if she enjoys it as much as he does. If this author's female character feels or thinks about anything at all, her feelings and thoughts are about him.

It was likely that I had requested this book at the time, so perhaps I had turned what is called a *blind eye* to all of this, or maybe there was something I wanted to find out. After all, I had brought it with me to the new shed. Yes, all these years later, there was something I still wanted to find out about writing character, in particular female character. After all, to think and feel and live and love more freely is the point of life, so it is an interesting project to construct a female character who has no life. The story in this book was about a woman who has *gifted* her life to a man. This is not something to be tried at home but it is usually where it happens.

How would a writer set about the massive task of giving a female character no consciousness, not even an unconscious life, as if it were the most normal thing in the world? Perhaps it was normal in *his* world. And yet it takes a lot of work to construct any sort of character in fiction. The writer and film director Céline Sciamma noted that when a female character is given subjectivity, she is given back her desires. It occurred to me that to create a female character with desires that were not just *his* own might have been something an author of his generation couldn't even *imagine*. In a sense, the *she* in his story was a missing female character. Her own desires were what were missing. For this reason, the author's book had been useful to me. Its lack of consciousness was a house I had attempted to dismantle in my own living and working life. Real estate is a tricky business. We rent and buy and sell and inherit it, but we also knock it down.

At this time, I found myself possessed by the ending in Elena Ferrante's novel *The Story of the Lost Child*, in which Lila, now in her late sixties, has disappeared without trace. From childhood to womanhood the lives of Lila and Lenù have been braided together, yet finally they are separated by Lila's disappearance. 'I loved Lila,' Lenù writes. 'I wanted her to last. But I wanted it to be I who made her last.' By the end of the book, Lila has become a missing female character.

As I sat in the chair by the window in my new writing shed, I asked myself why I was so interested in missing female characters? Perhaps I did not mean women who had literally gone missing (such as Lila) but who were missing their own desires.

And what about the women who had acted on their desires but then been cut down, their life *rewritten*, their existence retold to dilute their power and undermine their authority? Perhaps I was searching for a major *goddess* who, in the patriarchal rewrite of her existence, had become lost and gone missing?

I was thinking of Hecate at the crossroads with her burning torches and keys, Medusa with her snakes and fatal gaze, Artemis with her hunting dogs and deer, Aphrodite with her doves, Demeter with her mares, Athena with her owl. Whenever I saw eccentric and sometimes mentally fragile older women feeding pigeons on the pavement of every city in the world, I thought, *Yes, there she is, she is one of those cut-down goddesses who has become demented by life.*

Were the goddesses real estate owned by patriarchy?

Are women real estate owned by patriarchy?

And what about women who are rented for sex by men?

Who owns the deeds to the land in that transaction?

Most married, heterosexual male authors of my age were looked after by their wives at literary events. One of these men told me at a book festival that if he did not transgress too many boundaries in his marriage, there would always be a comforting pair of slippers warming for him by the fire. Thankfully, his wife managed to run away for a cigarette on the fire escape.

I regarded her invigorating conversation with me as much more interesting than any of the events I had attended at the festival. Many people in the audience would have enjoyed her thoughts on fragile tyrants, the ways in which love is altered by physical infidelity, and how she had dreamed her breasts were made from glass.

Would there ever be a comforting pair of slippers (pink, feathered) warming for me by the egg-shaped fireplace? Not unless I became a female character in a vintage Hollywood movie and paid a housekeeper to put them there. 'Mx Klimowski,' I would say, 'I believe in the morning my arthritic elbows will need to be massaged with oil of arnica.' *Very well, madame*. My housekeeper would be a character with many desires of their own because I was writing the script. I could see them leaning against the dusky-pink plaster walls of my real estate, wearing a brooch in the shape of a bee. *Your soup is ready. I have fed your wolves and prepared the smoking pipe with your desired brand of tobacco. By the way, madame* (my housekeeper's lips were stained from the raspberries they had devoured for lunch), *I note you are thinking about Real Estate. The word 'Real' derives from the Latin word 'Rex', meaning 'royal'. 'Real' also means 'king' in Spanish, because kings used to own all the land in their kingdoms. For Lacan, the Real is everything that cannot be said. It has nothing to do with reality. Is there anything else you require before I run my bath and listen to Lana Del Rey?*

'Yes, Mx Klimowski,' I would reply. 'If you could kindly prepare my plate of Turkish Delight – the rose and mandarin flavours are very pleasing.' *We have run out of the Delights, madame. May I suggest if you want a sweetmeat you get it your fucking self.*

They would retire to drink gin and have mystical visions and also pragmatic thoughts about how to make more money and buy a house of their own. Meanwhile, I would read the poetry of Sappho and Baudelaire by the egg-shaped fireplace while the phantom of love gently peeled an orange nearby.

> If I were asked to name the chief benefit of the house, I should say: the house shelters daydreaming, the house protects the dreamer, the house allows one to dream in peace.
>
> Gaston Bachelard,
> *The Poetics of Space* (1964)

I began to wonder what I and all the women missing their own desires and all the rewritten women (such as the goddesses) would possess in their property portfolios at the end of our lives. Including my imagined housekeeper, who at this moment is running their bath (a splash of rose and geranium oil) while listening to Lana Del Rey. What do we value (though it might not be societally valued), what might we own, discard and bequeath? If, like the great struggling goddesses, we were too powerful for the fathers and brothers of patriarchy, how did our repressed power and potency make itself manifest on a Monday? And indeed, if I was writing the script from start to finish, what did I want my female characters to value, own, discard and bequeath? Perhaps I was channelling Jane Austen, except the prospect of marriage was not a solution.

It was not lost on me that quite a few middle-class people my age had paid off their mortgages and owned at least one house elsewhere. I'd go to dinner parties and someone would announce they were leaving the next day for their pile in France or Italy – or, and this was the one that hurt most, they were off to write in a magical modernist pavilion specially built for them in the English countryside. Meanwhile, I was returning to the grim Corridors of Love, which still had not been repaired. There were some small improvements. I now owned not one electric bicycle but a fleet of electric bicycles. In this sense, as far as I was concerned, I resembled a rock star I knew who owned a fleet of aeroplanes. Yes, I had one e-bike locked up under the tree and two more in the garage. Friends came to stay from all over the world and we cycled around London together. It was a gesture towards a life I wanted, that is to say, an extended family of friends and their children, an expanded family rather than a nuclear family, which in this phase of my life seemed a happier way to live. If I wanted a spare room for every friend, my flat could not support this idea. If I wanted a fireplace in every room, there were no fireplaces in my flat. So what was I going to do with all this wanting?

*

I stared out at the very large garden in which my new shed was situated. Instead of buying some real estate, which I could not afford to do, perhaps I could gift my shed landlord a swimming pool, to be built on his land. I would then be able to write and swim and my lifestyle would have been achieved. I would own none of it but I could use it for as long as our friendship lasted. My daughters would swim in all weathers. What a gesture from their mother. What a gift to the landlord from his writer friend.

We would frolic in the water amongst the dragonflies and I would plant wild mint on the banks of the pool. I googled how much it would cost and came upon a site for eco pools. An hour passed. Eco pools were expensive. I realized my landlord might not want me to dig up his garden. I would have to put my imaginary spade down for the moment and get on with some work.

*

The second book I had brought with me to the new writing shed was a series of essays by various psychoanalysts, scholars and artists about one of my favourite film directors, Pedro Almodóvar.

In one chapter, Almodóvar describes the meaning of the phrase in Spanish *You are like a cow without a bell*. He explains, 'To be like a cow without a bell means being lost, without anyone taking any notice of you.' I thought I was a bit like a cow without a bell, but I was not lost. Maybe cows prefer not to have bells because they need to wander away from the field and from the threat of slaughter. The holy wandering cows I had encountered while strolling the streets of Ahmadabad, India, were very appealing to me. I liked to pat their backs and see the dust rise from their hides.

In the Hindu tradition, cows are a sacred animal. The mother sustains life with her milk and for this she is honoured and garlanded.

3

NEW YORK

At the end of May 2018, I was in New York, West Side Manhattan, to help clear out my deceased American stepmother's apartment.

My best male friend, who happened to be in New York at the time, offered to help. We had to figure where the local thrift shops were located and then go out on to the street, hail a yellow cab and ask the driver to take sixteen bags full of clothing to West 79th. The wrapping up of someone else's life (my stepmother was a distinguished academic) made me wonder if I should tear up my old diaries and throw away all the letters I had kept for decades? It was unbearably sad to see my stepmother's shirts, scarves and trousers neatly folded in drawers. I had agreed to clear out her closet to save my elderly father from the pain of doing this himself. He was very broken by her death, and when he phoned me from Cape Town (where she died) with the news, it was the first time in my life I had heard him cry.

There were two small glass jars full of buttons she had removed from various garments and saved to sew on to other garments. These buttons were the only things I kept for myself. Three of them were in the shape of white horses, their manes flying in the wind.

In my property portfolio so far, I owned a flat in my crumbling apartment block, three e-bikes and three wooden fairground horses from Afghanistan. I had bought these hand-painted horses from a dusty shop full of rugs and lamps in a desolate part of London when my children were young. The horses were big enough to seat a toddler. A friend told me they were 'antiques', possibly from the 1930s, but I did not know that when I bought them. To be antique suggests something old and dead, maybe even ghostly, but I was pulled towards these horses because they were so expressively alive. Somehow they signified freedom to me, and beauty too; each of the carved beasts had a very particular defiant mood. These horses, about two foot tall (two white, one black), now stood on the long windowsill in the crumbling apartment block on the hill. Sometimes I placed an avocado between their alert wooden ears when I wanted to ripen it. At Christmas my daughters and I garlanded their heads with holly and mistletoe. Everyone was pleased to kiss the horses (given the kissing rituals associated with mistletoe) but was also a little in awe of them. I thought that was right; after all, they were not cuddly toys. The man who parked his motorbike next to my e-bike in the back car park told me that every time he looked up and saw the horses in my window, he thought of them as my guard horses.

A woman I knew, who was abundantly wealthy and had never held down a job, wanted to buy my horses from me. There was only one time I nearly cracked, but in the end I could not part with the horses, which had, to my amazement, proved to be valuable in financial terms. It seemed that my Horses of Liberty were very much part of my property portfolio so far.

This woman told me that she never knew what to reply when working mothers asked her, 'What do you do?' I suggested she reply, 'I am an heiress.' That would probably end the conversations she found so awkward. And it did. It worked. It was true that being an heiress was her main job. All that money had to be looked after, as did her many properties. Her literal real estate was as vast as mine was tiny. She owned houses in Paris, Vienna, Paxos, Scotland, Spain and London. Most of her attention was focused on the upkeep of her properties, cooking vegan recipes, her three dogs and her vast orchard of olive trees in Spain. I thought she was an impressive woman in many ways. At least in winter she wore a beanie and not a green felt hat with a pheasant feather poking out of its ribbon. She was something of a Buddhist. A Buddhist with worldly riches, but with quite simple tastes. Sometimes when I met up with her she had saved a couple of perfect apricots in her pocket for our delectation, or a handful of almonds, or a wedge of hard regional Italian cheese for me to taste, given she was strictly vegan. She would slice it with the small penknife she kept in her purse, and then magically conjure up a couple of purple figs, which she said were friendly companions to the cheese. The heiress herself was a friendly companion.

Apparently, her husband, who was from Naples but who was not vegan, knew how to plait mozzarella, braiding three strings of this milky cheese together for feast days. The process of making mozzarella, she explained, is called *pasta filata*, and the favoured milk is from the water buffalo. This had me wondering if water buffalo should be honoured and garlanded like the holy cows in India, but I preferred to think of them ecstatically submerged in swamps, rivers and ponds.

I did not share with her my everyday problems or my dream of owning a grand old house with a pomegranate tree in the garden. She was an heiress after all. My life and living were too distant from her experience of life and living, but I respected the intelligent and playful way she handled her own turbulent family problems.

*

Every Christmas I bought olive oil from the heiress to give to my friends as gifts. This oil, from her farm in Andalusia, was the elixir of life, green and peppery, startling to taste. She told me it was 'first-press oil', often called virgin oil, and she combed it through her hair every Friday. Each olive released only one or two drops of oil, so, she said, imagine how many olives are needed to make just one kilo of oil? Sometimes I would sprinkle sea salt on a wedge of sour green tomato and dip it into the peppery emerald olive oil. It was as if I had struck on something good that was within my reach.

I was fond of the heiress and not that envious of her real estate. This lack of envy (given that every one of her many villas came very close to the home of my dreams) frankly surprised me. In a way, she had so many homes that she was homeless. Every month she seemed to be travelling between her properties across a number of countries. When she rang my mobile there was always another dialling code on my screen. Although my flat was small and humble, it was certainly my home, our home, our perch in the sky, though I needed some Buddhism to help me endure the grey communal corridors. The owners of the freehold had recently mended frays and tears in the old carpets outside the lift with blue masking tape. For this repair they sent enormous service-charge bills. All the same, it was encouraging to stare out at the sky and know that everything is always changing, that a dark sky lifts into another mood.

Meanwhile, here I was in New York trying not to combust while clearing out my stepmother's flat, which was much swankier than my own. I thought about how little I knew about her life before she met my father. Now I was sifting through her shower caps, cardigans, berets, nightdresses, umbrellas, various boxes of make-up and hair curlers. In a way I was getting to know her better, which was sad and weird. When my own mother died, it was my younger brother who had done most of the heavy lifting in this regard. I now realized he had saved me the misery of this awful task. I think he knew me better than anyone else, because I once overheard him say to a woman who asked why his sister (me) liked to work in a shed, 'I think she likes a feral space to write.'

My contribution to the aftermath of my mother's death had been to register this very shocking death with the town hall and to collect her ashes from the funeral parlour. The registering was the worst part because when it was my turn to sign various documents, the clerk called out my mother's name as if she were alive. The effect of this was to have me in tears before I even entered the clerk's office, so perhaps my brother reckoned he might have an easier time going through my mother's clothes alone. He suggested I choose some of the many books on her shelves. When I brought them home, the pages were yellow and dusty, stained and sticky, and, worse, some of the sentences were underlined and she had written comments in the margins. How could I throw away her ghostly thoughts speaking to me from these decaying books?

On the third day in New York, I met a hefty man in the lift with his golden Labrador. He told me how his dog, Goldie (that was the name of my aunt as well), had got her tail stuck in the lift door. He said he started to scream and cry and his dog was wailing too (while I was listening I was hoping this was going to have a happy ending) but then the lift stopped at Floor 4 (there were twenty-one floors) and yes, all was well. Goldie's tail was freed, no damage. I looked at Goldie's tail. It looked a bit forlorn, as if it had been through something big.

There was a young woman standing in the lift with us, holding two takeout iced coffees from Starbucks. They were topped with swirls of cream and chocolate chips. She told us she was looking forward to the sugar rush. Actually, she said, it was an everything rush that she was looking forward to. When I told that to my best male friend, he said he wanted an everything rush too. That was a great project to aim for in life, he said, to be an Everything Rush.

Later in the day, taking a break from cleaning the apartment (dust on my *eyelashes*), I saw an African American woman walking her cat on the Manhattan sidewalk. It was a silvery long-haired cat, wearing a silver collar. The woman was dressed in a crop top with inked drawings of eyes all over her breasts and platform cream-coloured shoes with painted swirls on the toes. What with her cat and shoes and the painted eyes on her T-shirt, I thought that she was an Everything Rush.

It was a shock to be lugging a distinguished woman's shoes to her local thrift shop, including a brand-new pair of trainers, still wrapped in tissue inside their box. To calm down I walked to Central Park. It had suddenly become warm and I was so jet-lagged I thought I might faint. I found a place near the entrance to the park under a tree and collapsed on to the grass. Lying on my back, looking up at the big American sky between the leaves, I saw something hanging from the branches. It was a key. A key on a red ribbon that someone had hung on a branch and forgotten to take with them. At first, I was sorry for the person who had forgotten to take the key. Then I wondered if they had deliberately left it behind because they were never going to return to wherever the key belonged. Or perhaps they wanted to close a door on a chapter of their life and leaving the key behind was a gesture of this desire. There is always something secret and mysterious about keys. They are the instrument to enter and exit, open and close, lock and unlock various desirable and undesirable domains.

I had spent so much of my life peering into the windows of estate agents, searching for my very own domain, my face pressed against the window, along with the ghosts of other dreamers looking for homes we could not afford. Nevertheless, I believed that one day, when I grew up, I would earn myself the keys to a house of my own in the Mediterranean with honeysuckle and balconies. At the same time a mean little voice in my head was always saying, 'This is not real, it will never be yours.'

*

Yes, I had spent a long time trying to have a more bourgeois life. Somehow it seemed hard to get one. My colleagues who really did have well-developed bourgeois lives were always trying to be less bourgeois, but I wanted to move into the neighbourhood.

Bonjour, isn't the air a delight here! Look at our country cottages with their tangle of pink climbing roses. Look at the lake we made from natural springs. Look! Look on Twitter: our ducks are sleeping under the willow trees! Look at our dining table and its constellation of chairs, look at the art on our walls, our pergola, our salad bowls and oriental poppies, our Victorian porcelain and wild-flower meadows. Look at this slice of buttered toast next to the modernist lamp. Look! Look at you looking on Instagram! Here we are, setting off on our country walk with Molly, our sweet-natured Burmese python!

*

If real estate is a self-portrait and a class portrait, it is also a body arranging its limbs to seduce. Actually, I couldn't work out why real estate wasn't flirting with me more intensely, its swooning eyes making me all kinds of offers I couldn't refuse. After all, I was at last able to live from my writing. As I lay beneath the abandoned or forgotten key in Central Park and started to think about all this, it was too depressing to linger on the real and pragmatic reasons for still living in the wreck of the London apartment block.

I had started writing in my early twenties and was first published age twenty-seven, though my plays were performed throughout my early twenties. It has been immensely powerful putting words into the mouths of actors, but it was hard to pay the bills. I thought about the writer Rebecca West, whose books had brought her enough wealth at forty to buy herself a Rolls-Royce and a grand country house, or *estate*, in the Chiltern Hills. At the age of forty my second daughter was three months old and I was experimenting with how to make dhal (very cheap) from a variety of pulses and lentils. While Rebecca West put her foot down in her new swanky car, I was figuring how to combine spices and whether it would be better to serve dhal with rice or learn how to make roti and other Indian flatbreads, which I did: brown wheat flour, water, oil, ghee. Yes, it gave me such pleasure to see how the dough bubbled and puffed up in the frying pan and to simmer butter and strain it. Later I went on to make paratha, much trickier: it required pleating the dough. I couldn't believe it. I was making delicious dhal and rotis and parathas to feed my family and I was writing through the night, familiar with every car alarm that went off at four in the morning. At the same age, Rebecca West was parking her new Rolls-Royce in the grounds of her real estate in the Chiltern Hills and Camus was receiving the Nobel Prize.

> Only part of us is sane: only part of us loves pleasure and the longer day of happiness, wants to live to our nineties and die in peace, in a house that we built, that shall shelter those who come after us. The other half of us is nearly mad. It prefers the disagreeable to the agreeable, loves pain and its darker night despair, and wants to die in a catastrophe that will set back life to its beginnings and leave nothing of our house save its blackened foundations.
>
> Rebecca West, *Black Lamb and Grey Falcon* (1941)

I was with Rebecca West some of the way, but not with the blackened foundations. If you are not wealthy, you do not want a catastrophe in which your house burns down. My horses! My wok! My little lamp fringed with white pom-poms! All the same, those invisible years raising our children and getting to grips with all those parathas were some of the most formative years of my life. I didn't know it then, but I was becoming the writer I wanted to be. I was going to step into her and she was going to step into me. I was pleased I was not wearing the equivalent of sensible shoes to write the stories, novels and plays that preoccupied me in my twenties. I was finding a way through the forest (wearing silver platform boots) to meet the wolf. Who or what is the wolf? Perhaps the wolf is the whole point of writing.

To walk towards danger, to strike on something that might just open its mouth and roar and tip the writer over the edge was part of the adventure of language. Anyone who thinks deeply, freely and seriously will move nearer to life and death and everything else we pass on the way. Any cleaner getting up at dawn to sweep offices, railway stations, schools, hospitals, will be familiar with this sort of thinking.

She knows she has to be stronger than her most fearful thoughts, stronger than her exhaustion. It is likely there are many people who hear and see her, though she might not be visible on Instagram (*Look! Look at the hours I work! Look at my three jobs! Look at my hands!*) but that doesn't stop her from thinking big thoughts. Thought *is* language. Avoiding thought *is* language. I once taught a writing class just looking at the words *Yes* and *No*. We agreed that a sign on a gate that reads *No Blacks, No Jews, No Gypsies* is the most impoverished language of all. The signs on public swimming pools in the 1970s were interesting texts, too. *No Diving, No Petting, No Eating, No Splashing.* Why not put up a sign that just says *No. No. No.* And what would happen if we were to flip the sign? *Yes. Yes. Yes.*

Yes. I wanted a house. And a garden. I wanted land.

The key hanging in the branches of that tree in Central Park opened the doors to many other houses in my mind.

I was aware that James Baldwin had spent the last seventeen years of his life living in the French town of Saint-Paul-de-Vence. As I understood it, he rented a stone house with orange trees and palms and views of the sea and the mountains. It was his refuge from hostility to his skin colour and homosexuality in 1970s America. He wrote in this rented stone house, ashtray on his desk, the fireplace behind his chair. Miles Davis, Stevie Wonder, Nina Simone, Ella Fitzgerald: all made the journey to visit him. He talked long into the warm, Mediterranean night with friends, seated around a table in the garden. His former Swiss lover lived in the gatehouse with his family and nursed Baldwin when he became sick from stomach cancer. Apparently, Baldwin took steps to buy this house when he was dying, but somehow it did not work out. After his death, his rented real estate did not become the James Baldwin Museum. I, for one, would have made the pilgrimage just to see the glass ashtray on his desk. I would have liked to glimpse where he wrote and thought and welcomed friends. The house was not just a domestic space, it was a political space. He'd had to leave his country and make a kinder world in a house he had rented elsewhere. It was not the first time he had to escape racism in America to survive and to write. He had arrived in Paris from New York in the winter of 1948 with forty dollars in his pocket. At that time, he lived in a crummy hotel in the Rue de Verneuil. A rented house on the Côte d'Azur with orange and palm trees in the courtyard, surrounded by friends, was an encouraging image. I had kept it in my head for decades, like an old photograph in my family album.

*

I glanced again at the key hanging from the branch. Should I hand it in to someone in the park who dealt with lost property? No. If I had lost a key, I would eventually remember where I left it and return to the tree (panicking) to claim it.

I did not want to return to open the door of my stepmother's now empty apartment, so I spent the rest of the day at a hotel that I knew had a pool on its rooftop. I was wearing my swimming costume under my dress, so it seemed this was an assignment waiting to happen. It was humid. Three small military planes flew in formation above the pool. A DJ was busy setting up his deck. He was a skinny white guy dressed in denim and gold spectacles. Young attractive women and men lazed on sun loungers. It was a freakishly hot day. I put on some shades and tried not to fall asleep. At first the DJ played soul. The Hudson was nearby. And the High Line. A mangy banana tree was trying to grow in a pot near the bar.

My own banana tree was much healthier. In fact it was flourishing in North London and now almost four feet tall. My daughter had just sent me a photograph of it and promised she was watering the third child every day.

I ordered a Bloody Mary. It arrived with two giant olives pierced on a stick and inside the olives were two gherkins. Even a giant olive is small, so the gherkins were miniature. The celery stick was the size of a baby's arm. While I was figuring out the scale of all the trimmings that accompanied my Bloody Mary, a man about my age arrived with his two young daughters. The DJ was playing a song with the chorus *I want to sex you up*. The father was sent away because kids were not allowed on the roof terrace after 11.30. One daughter had neon-orange water wings strapped to her arms; the other wore a kind of wetsuit with nylon fish scales and a full mermaid's tail. It was the first time I had seen a mermaid with legs and a tail. It was a clever design. I suppose having legs and a mermaid's tail can be described as having it all.

I also wanted to swim in the tiny pool but didn't think I could bear the shame of doing the lengths in my black Speedo costume, observed by the lean, gorgeous men and women sipping mojitos perched on the edge of the pool. It was only four feet deep, as tall as my banana plant. After a while I dived in, two legs, no tail.

On the way back to my stepmother's apartment I discovered a market. One of the stalls sold deep-fried Oreos. I bought sunglasses for my daughters, also a pair for my best male friend and some cumin and paprika for his wife, Nadia, who liked to cook with these spices. While I was searching my bag for dollars, a woman wearing a flamboyant coat came up to me. She told me she loved my brogues with their big black and white tongues. She was Brooklyn, she said, so not to mess with her, but she wanted to tell me that she herself had seven pairs of her own brogues, two in a colour she described as 'tomato', one in lemon yellow and four in various shades of blue, from sky blue to night blue. They didn't sound like brogues to me at all. She told me she was a digital director of something and that her husband was a doctor and then she walked away. It was so strange. I couldn't work out why she had given me this information, but I reckoned she would have many pairs of shoes in her property portfolio. I hoped she would bequeath them to someone who liked them, given that I had just carried all my stepmother's shoes in a garbage bag to the thrift shop.

When I returned to the apartment in Manhattan, my best male friend noted that he had been mopping the floors of every room while

I had been swimming in a pool on a rooftop, knocking back a Bloody Mary and then rounding off the day with a dash of market shopping.

'Why don't I make you an Everything Rush?' I said, my hair still wet from the pool. As I passed him a glass of strong cold coffee, he shook his head mournfully.

'I think it suffers from lack of sugar, to be frank. It's not an Everything Rush, just a caffeine rush.' While he complained I told him about the key on the branch of the tree in Central Park.

'In some ways,' he said, 'you are like my wife. She's also obsessed with keys. Except she's happy and pretends to be unhappy and you're unhappy and pretend to be happy.' He rattled the ice in his disappointing caffeine rush and then he tugged at his right earlobe, something he always did when he was about to say something provocative.

'Your youngest is leaving home soon so

you might as well consider hooking up with someone to share your life.'

When he'd stopped fondling his ear, he actually wiggled his eyebrows for emphasis.

The next morning as I made my way to Fairway to buy a melon for our breakfast, I saw a woman feeding pigeons on the sidewalk. I wondered if throwing seeds to the pigeons was her way of feeling valued and loved. Perhaps she would be an interesting major female character instead of a minor character and I should propose this to the film executives next time we met. When I saw she had painted on her eyebrows so that one was much higher than the other, I suddenly felt exhausted and didn't think I could commit to the slog and sorrow of her back story. I saw her as a child with both eyebrows in the right place, but knew I would have to track the long female journey to the left eyebrow floating near her hairline. As a structure for a film, that was quite appealing. I was also thinking about my best male friend's idea that his wife, Nadia, was happy but pretended to be unhappy. Why did he think she was pretending?

4

LONDON

I had become obsessed with silk. I wanted to sleep in it and wear it and somehow knew it had healing properties. It started when a royalty cheque came in and I took it literally and began to sleep like royalty. First, I bought a silk double duvet cover and a sheet, then six pil-low cases, the colour of turmeric. To sleep in silk was a revelation. It was cool and warm, like a second skin, perhaps like a lover. When I replaced the silk with the cotton sheet on which I had slept all my life, it suddenly felt very harsh on my skin. I kept it there for a week, perhaps in the way that hair shirts were worn as a means of keeping in touch with the harsh realities of life. Frankly, I did not need any more of that sort of reality. In this regard the silk sheets were lighter than the weight of my living.

I was hospitable to this strange desire for silk, but couldn't work out what was going on. I truly thought I might be dying. Perhaps I was psychically preparing to be embalmed in silk like an ancient Egyptian pharaoh. Yes, it would be very appealing to be embalmed in silk, myrrh, beeswax and resins, or to be preserved in a paste of charcoal and clay. In fact I would have liked all those things while I was still living, preferably mixed together in a face mask.

Apparently, Xin Zhui from China's Han dynasty (also known as Lady Dai) had been wrapped in twenty layers of silk when she died in 163 BC. Best of all, 138 melon seeds were found in her throat, stomach and intestines. I liked to think of her wrapped in silk on a summer's day while she enjoyed a slice of juicy melon. Her body was found intact, which was a relief. I did not want my brain scooped out of my skull with an iron hook, pharaoh style, though I wanted his status.

I discovered that silkworms feed on mulberry leaves and that mulberries contain a high level of antioxidants, which aid cellular repair in the body. Well then. I should get a fleet of silkworms of my own and employ an entourage to tend them for my silk habit. Electric bikes, wooden horses and silkworms would be part of my property portfolio. Best of all, I learned that silk is made in the salivary glands of silkworms. A kind of glandular fever of silk. I also read that the mother of singer/actress Jane Birkin advised her daughter: 'When you've got nothing left . . . get into silk underwear and start reading Proust.'

Perhaps now that I was separated from the father of my daughters and the youngest would be departing in the autumn, I had nothing left? Whatever, if I was going to channel a pharaoh I wanted some sacred animals to be buried with me. That thought was very comforting. I would have to leave a note about this in my will. I could see my daughters reading it in a fury: 'Well, she's not having the cat, no, Lulu will live another day to catch birds and purr on our laps.' My older daughter, who had a skill for killer punchlines that often made me laugh for days, would mutter, 'The things we have to do' and then add another lethal, perfect sentence of her own.

My Norwegian friend, Agnes, came over for a spritz cocktail. She wore sparkling green earrings that were almost as blinding as her very white teeth. It was 6pm and we'd both just finished work. A fierce wind was blowing through London. The weather-forecast people had named it Storm Eleanor. No doubt about it, Eleanor was rattling the Crittal windows of the crumbling apartment block in quite an assertive way. At one point Agnes and I thought she might even crack the glass.

I made the spritz with Prosecco, Campari, a dash of tonic and a slice of orange. It was a summer drink, but as Camus said of himself, there was an eternal summer inside me, even when a storm was threatening to topple my building.

'You've even chilled the glasses,' Agnes said, examining the frosted crystal flutes I had bought in Vienna when I was on a book tour there. I told her I had learned this trick from my best male friend. He always chilled the glasses in the freezer for margaritas, an attempt to make his third wife happy.

Actually, Nadia preferred smoothies made from kale and celery.

When I'd finally achieved my grand old

house with the pomegranate tree, I would have a separate freezer just for chilling glasses. Recently I had replaced the fountains in the grounds of this house with a river at the end of the garden. My unreal estate now included a small rowing boat tied to the jetty of this river. My friends would drop by and find me sanding and varnishing the oars of my boat, feet dangling in the cool clear water. Were there fish in that river? Definitely. What kind of fish? I had not yet got to the stage of identifying them, because I had only recently replaced the fountains with a whole tidal river. And what was the name of the boat? It would be called *Sister Rosetta*, after the African American singer Sister Rosetta Tharpe, the godmother of rock and roll, gospel's first female electric-guitar superstar. She had long been my role model for middle age, ever since I saw a film of her performing when she was forty-nine in a railway station in Manchester. Her electric guitar slung over her high-collared coat and her glamorous stiletto-heeled shoes were just up my street. Chuck Berry and Elvis and Little Richard had all learned a trick from Sister Rosetta. In the film, a friend had said of the force and beauty of her voice, 'She could make you cry, and then she made you want to dance.' I would enjoy painting her name on my boat. When I told all this to Agnes, she said, 'I just don't get why you want a house in the wilderness. You are a cosmopolitan sort of person, you like dressing up and going to parties, you like heeled shoes and high-collared coats like Sister Rosetta, in fact you get your best ideas when you're in a crowd, so why have you gone rural? I mean, you're a diva, you always have been.'

I had not yet told her about the silk sheets.

Agnes sipped the spritz and declared it tip-top. While Eleanor howled through the dilapidated building, I noticed that Agnes had more poise than when we'd last met. Her body had changed. She seemed taller, softer, she smiled more often. Since she'd separated from Ruth, her long-time partner, she told me she had started to feel things again. Sometimes this was good, other times bad. She glanced at the horses on my windowsill, her eyes stormy blue like the deep Scandinavian fjords near where she was born.

Apparently, Ruth had told her she was always on her 'high horse' and wanted to pull her off it. The high horse. The high horse. It was always good to see a woman on her high horse. Why had Ruth wanted to take her down? To where? How low? Why bother to pull a woman off her high horse? Storm Ruth.

I think the high horse is supposed to suggest arrogance, or superiority, but I believed in this case it really meant that Agnes had a sense of her own purpose in life, that she got on with the things she wanted to do in the world, which is sometimes called agency or holding the reins of the high horse and steering it. After all, there is no point in climbing on to a high horse if you don't know how to ride it. I was fascinated with the *high horse* and especially when a woman wanted to pull another woman off it. Ruth had spent a long time undermining Agnes and a short time loving her. They were thirty-six when they met and forty-seven when they parted. That was a lot of life, so obviously the horses had come out to play.

Agnes told me that since she had moved out of the house she had shared with her former partner, she had a very weird desire to wear real emerald earrings.

'I yearned for some rocks.'

She explained that she did not want

emeralds to make any sort of statement about wealth (she was not wealthy), no, what she wanted in middle age were stones that had come from deep within the earth and that sparkled on her ears. She needed *lustre*. She would gaze into the windows of jewellers and think, *No, those ones are too small*, even though she could not afford emeralds the size of a pinhead lying in their little velvet coffins. We wondered if rocks cut out of the earth were somehow connected to blood and bone and the beginning of time. But then I pointed out that she did not want to wear coal on her ears, and coal was also hewn out of the earth.

'So anyway,' she continued, pointing to her ears, 'these will do for the time being.' She had bought herself green crystal earrings that were an imitation of the emeralds she wanted to glitter on her ears. Yes, she would have *lustre* as she rode her high horse down the North Circular to repair her smashed screen at Mr Cellfone.

I reckoned it was time to tell her about the silk sheets, and when I did, she insisted on having a look at them.

Turmeric. Golden.

'I think you have gone home to the country of your birth,' she suggested. I told her I would add the silk to my property portfolio, along with the horses and the e-bikes. She noticed a lamp made from wood and copper on my desk and thought it worth including in the inventory, along with my library of books by Sigmund Freud and the poetry of Apollinaire.

Storm Eleanor had calmed down.

'The odd thing,' she told me, as we walked back to the bottle of Prosecco in the living room, 'is that people tell me I look like a queen in my faux emeralds.' It was true that in her phase of new poise, she looked quite majestic.

I asked her if a queen was a good thing to be?

'Yes, it is,' she said. 'It's strange, but why not? Someone who commands attention. Someone who is entitled, who is required to be listened to.'

I suggested that if she were a queen it was likely she grew up in a castle and sat astride a childhood rocking horse with a leather saddle. That was not the same as being on a high horse, though it might be a rehearsal for the real thing. There would be paintings of patriarchs on the stone walls of the castle and she would not have been cuddled, tickled or kissed by her royal parents in case too much affection harmed her character. While I spoke, her new rocks sparkled and caught the light.

I did not tell Agnes I was thinking about the White Queen and the Red Queen, also the

Queen of Hearts in Lewis Carroll's *Through the Looking-Glass.* One of those queens always had a brush stuck in her hair. Apparently, the English illustrator John Tenniel struck on this idea from watching distraught female patients in the insane asylums of his time. A common delusion shared by these women was that they were queens. Lewis Carroll had given some thought to the psychology of these mature, raging women:

> I pictured to myself the Queen of Hearts as a sort of embodiment of ungovernable passion – a blind and aimless Fury.
>
> The Red Queen I pictured as a Fury, but of another type; *her* passion must be cold and calm; she must be formal and strict, yet not unkindly; pedantic to the tenth degree, the concentrated essence of all governesses!

Jane Eyre was a governess but she was not cold and calm. Charlotte Brontë had rewritten the script. Her governess was not a forbidding maternal character, in fact she was motherless herself and had no idea how to be a stern mother to an adult man she desired. Jane Eyre's alter ego (Bertha Rochester), conveniently locked in the attic, was an embodiment of ungovernable passion, a sort of Queen of Hearts. Perhaps she had a hairbrush stuck in her hair, too. The mad woman in the attic had refused to be governed by her husband.

I began to wonder if the delusion of being queen, or, in my case, a pharaoh, was about acquiring power and respect, just as Agnes had described. In this sense, perhaps there was not so much difference between a queen and a woman who feeds pigeons on the pavement. They both apparently had devoted subjects bowing at their feet, some human, some feathered.

Agnes's hair was very sleek. It did not have

a hairbrush stuck in it. Maybe she was more like Juno, the patron goddess of the Roman Empire, who was named 'Regina', or Queen. Juno wore a diadem on her head and was often pictured sitting with a peacock close to her feet. I made a note of this peacock to torment future film executives. When I was next asked to come up with ideas for a potential leading female character, I would say, 'How about she sits in her humble London flat eating cornflakes with a peacock sitting at her feet?'

We finished the spritz and I made a pot of spaghetti with anchovies to accompany the next round. Both of us had been watching a TV drama series titled *Feud*, about the lives and careers of Bette Davis and Joan Crawford and, indeed, their ongoing spat. Apparently, Bette Davis (played by Susan Sarandon) had the talent and Joan Crawford (Jessica Lange) had the looks. They were both single mothers and divas and alcoholics. Storm Bette. Storm Joan.

Out of the two of them, Crawford was scripted as being least able to accept ageing with grace and ease. She knew her fading looks would put her out of work and that is exactly what happened.

As these actresses aged, the roles available to them began to shrink. All the emeralds and silk sheets in the world, even the best make-up artists in town, were not going to get them major roles again. That is to say, the kinds of roles in which they were desired by their various male leads. The parts they were offered were mothers, grandmothers, and in Crawford's case a hokey female scientist in a movie called *Trog*. When I looked up *Trog*, I could see the appeal. At least Crawford's character, Dr Brockton, has a profession, and when she finds an Ice Age caveman, sets about making him her pet. It is well documented that middle-aged and older female actors suddenly discover there are no roles for them to play on stage and in film. This was not news to me, but watching Bette and Joan experience exactly the same problems as their sisters in the twenty-first century began to preoccupy me.

I asked Agnes why playing mothers, grandmothers, great-aunts and eccentric spinsters was seen as a demotion? It occurred to me that what was wrong with the scripts was that the mothers and grandmothers were always there to police the more interesting desires of others, or to comfort them, or to be wise and dull.

The more eccentric older women were there to provide comedy. These sorts of characters were mostly unattached to men. There were no female characters who had full lives of their own – particularly lives in which they felt content. No, they were portrayed as looking after their elderly husbands, or they were lonely, bereft of company, or sick and ailing, or they were tyrants in the domestic sphere, or they were mad.

Why were they written like that? It was clear to me that Gertrude Stein and Alice Toklas had enjoyed a far better life in their later years than Bette Davis and Joan Crawford. Agnes poked my arm with her fork. I think she was reminding me about being dragged off her high horse by Ruth.

I wondered how I would write a script for Bette Davis and Joan Crawford in middle and old age. How would the story unfold? No cranky eccentric stuff. Alright, maybe a desire for silk sheets and emeralds. Agnes was busy picking the anchovies out of her spaghetti. I had to explain that it was in fact an anchovy spaghetti, so all she would have left was spaghetti.

'What about loneliness?' she said. 'I am very lonely right now.'

'Yes,' I replied, 'give her loneliness. Even better, give her a critique of her loneliness. Give her desires and conflicts that are not all about men. Give her melancholy rather than depression, sadness rather than despair. Why would a melancholy female character not be likeable?'

Agnes was looking despairingly into her spaghetti.

'Give her everything except anchovies,' I said, waving my hands around. 'Give her the goats sleeping in the argan trees west of Marrakesh.'

Agnes confessed she was baffled. The look on her face was similar to that of the film executives.

I had recently been watching Ingmar Bergman's film *Through a Glass Darkly*, a dark tale (obviously) about a family vacation on the

Swedish island of Fårö. The father character is a writer. He is lonesome, detached, self-involved, sad. He buys his children thoughtless gifts they do not want. He is never around for his adult daughter and son but they want him to be there for them. He is driven by his vocation and is still writing at four in the morning on his family holiday. His grown-up children disturb him with their problems while he works. They want his admiration and attention. Yes, he has charisma, he is a deep thinker and they all want a piece of him. The gentle son-in-law, married to the father's mentally fragile daughter, tells this father character (as they take a trip out on a boat) that his callousness in pursuing his own interests and obsessions over the needs of his family is perverse. That he knows nothing of life, that he is a coward and a genius at evasion and excuses.

The father character weeps alone in the kitchen and then puts his social face on and rejoins the family as if nothing has happened. Reality terrifies him, the humdrum of everyday life bores him, the frailties of his children distress him. Most of all he is envious and baffled by the enduring love his son-in-law feels for his suffering daughter. After all, he himself has many lovers who come and go, and takes up flattering offers to work abroad – yes, he will leave his family to make art about the human condition, away from his kin, but nevertheless connected to them.

He is a truly fascinating character. What was likeable was Bergman's critique of his leading male character. The way he allowed him to mess up, to be foolish and profound, kind and cruel, to exist with full complexity and paradox.

'Well, how about a *female* character who exists like that?' I had recently suggested to three film executives, two of them women.

They all looked a bit strained but leaned forward to hear more.

I noted the way they leaned forward and hoped I was on the brink of finally selling them a script. 'Yes,' I said, 'she follows all her desires, every single one of them. She is ruthless in pursuit of her vocation, takes up every job offer while her family pine for her. Furthermore,' I said, 'she has many affairs with people she will never fully commit to and she always buys her children thoughtless, last-minute presents at the airport when she returns from her exciting travels.'

The kindest female executive laughed. She looked exhausted. There were dark rings under her eyes. Perhaps I was exhausting her. Perhaps her family were exhausting her. Earlier, before the meeting had formally begun, she had been telling me about sleepless nights with her new baby. I did not want to have this conversation with her because I was there to pitch ideas that would buy me some real estate. The cruellest female executive asked me how the audience were supposed to like such a character?

'It's a hard call,' I replied.

I guessed that no woman around that table had ruthlessly pursued her own dreams and desires at the expense of everyone else. In fact I knew we felt guilty every time we absented ourselves from the wishes and desires of those who depend on us for their well-being and for cashflow.

There were many women I knew, including myself, who were not dependent on others, but depended on, for cashflow. Those people who relied on the talents of others were often resentful and hostile. They wanted to pull these women off her high horse, but their own bread and butter depended on her skilfully steering the high horse and galloping into the big bad world to pay the mortgage for them.

So then, what did the executives want their female characters to be like? I should have asked that question, but I already knew the answer. They had to be likeable.

Is a woman steering her high horse, with desires of her own, likeable?

Only if she steers her horse off the cliff. She is allowed to be exceptionally skilled at dying.

Another scene from the Bergman film came to mind. The intense father character smokes a pipe outside at night while looking dreamily at the stars. His children sit by his feet, waiting for him to say something incredible. Unfortunately, this scene gave me another idea to present to the executives. 'Perhaps this intense female mother/writer character looks dreamily up at the stars while her children sit at her feet, waiting for her to say something incredible.' They knew I knew this was ridiculous, but somehow they could not laugh with me. After all, who and what would we be laughing about?

The coolest male executive sort of smiled. Then he looked at his phone. My potential real estate had turned to dust before my eyes. I could have built a mansion from that dust alone. The female character I was describing would be a subversive character, but if he were a male character he would not be subversive. This meeting had been held in a London media club. When I signed in at the desk, the young woman at reception had said, 'Oh, are you the writer?' and when I said yes, she had astute things to say about a particular novel I had written and which she had enjoyed. I truly wanted to call her up to this meeting and beg her to stand in for me while I worked her shift.

At the very least, I told Agnes, I never wanted to see a film again in which a man in his late fifties is romantically involved with a woman in her early twenties and for this gap in the season of their lives to never be referred to from her point of view. It's true that in Bergman's film I did wonder why the gentle middle-aged son-in-law attempts to have sex with his beautiful young schizophrenic wife. After all, she is unwell and recovering from brutal electric shock treatment. She pushes him away, apologizes for her lack of wanting him, runs upstairs to the attic and walks through the wall to another sort of life. This is supposed to be a hallucination, part of her illness, but maybe another sort of life is exactly what she most wants.

*

Agnes and I talked late into the night. Whenever she moved her head, the green crystal earrings sent prisms of light around the room, like a glitter ball at a disco. She suggested that if I wanted to buy my grand old house, I should come up with a likeable female character who marries the male lead by the end of the film. Be pragmatic, she insisted, nail the deal, write the script and acquire your house with the river and the rowing boat.

I glanced at the horses on the windowsill. They stared back with their sombre painted eyes.

'Well then,' Agnes said, slipping off her shoes and moving from her chair to the rug on the floor, 'I don't think you really want your house with the river and the rowing boat.' She told me where she kept her cigarettes. I took one from her bag and lit it with her lighter, which was tucked into a secret zipped pocket.

'No, you are quite wrong, Agnes,' I said while I blew out smoke. 'I want that house more than anything else. I want the deeds to that house.' While I smoked, Agnes began to try out a yogic headstand. When she was perfectly aligned, up went her long Scandinavian legs, her toes now pointing towards the ceiling.

'In fact,' I said, 'I have been carrying that house inside me all my life.'

'It must be very heavy then,' Agnes replied. 'Why not let it go?'

I waved my cigarette at her feet. 'Never! I would fall apart without that house to look forward to.'

Agnes, who was still upside down, was now doing some sort of starfish movement with her legs. No. It was a scissor movement and she was busy cutting my real-estate dreams to shreds.

'Get off your high horse, Agnes,' I shouted through a coil of smoke.

'You know,' she said, 'I think your spritz has improved my balance.'

It was true that even when she was upside down, her green crystal earrings gave her a kind of majesty.

5

MUMBAI

It is the task of the translator to release in his own language that pure language which is under the spell of another, to liberate the language imprisoned in a work in his re-creation of that work.

Walter Benjamin, *Illuminations: Essays and Reflections* (1968)

As my books began to be translated across the world, I never lost the thrill of seeing my words laid out on the page in another language. Many writers I knew had been translated when they were much younger than me, so travelling to meet their readers had become part of their professional lives. In business terms I was about eight years old. As it happens, that was the age I started writing. When I was eight, I invented a cat that was neither he nor she. It could fly and do arabesques above a row of jacaranda trees. It had yellow eyes and its immense power scared me. That was a good thing. What is the point of writing a story that makes you chuckle and eventually doze off? In that story, I discovered the cat was lonely despite its power. In my late teens, the first translated book I read in the suburbs of London was *One Hundred Years of Solitude*. I thought about that childhood cat when I read how Colonel Aureliano Buendía was lonely and lost precisely because he had such immense power.

> Lost in the solitude of his immense power,
> he began to lose direction.

That sentence lit up my life in West Finchley. The epic poetry of Gabriel García Márquez had been delivered to the surburbs of England by a heroic, invisible translator. Did it ever occur to me that one day I might write a book that would be translated and read by someone living in the suburbs of another country? Although that seemed way beyond the reach of a teenage girl in the 1970s, I began to get a sense of the magnitude of the world and wanted to dive into it.

To be *translated* was like living another life in another body in France, Ukraine, Sweden, Vietnam, Germany, China, the Czech Republic, Spain, Romania – wherever. I often thought about my translators, mostly unknown to me, though some did email questions, often strange questions. Sometimes my word choices had to be changed because they had three other meanings in another language and culture. I knew these skilled translators were not creating a doppelgänger of my book, so much as a new life for it. Reaching out into the big, bewildering world was the point of writing, in fact it was the only point. At the same time Brexit devoured the news and I was anxiously wondering what life separated from Europe would be like. Maybe it would be like living in a kind of silence.

> Without translation we would inhabit parishes bordering on silence.
>
> George Steiner, *Errata: An Examined Life* (1997)

I said goodbye to my daughters because I had been invited to a literary festival in Mumbai, India. On the plane, preparing to sleep, I sprinkled a few drops of lavender oil on to my pillow. When I woke up twenty minutes later, I tried a drop of ylang-ylang to conjure up the sleep that had evaded me. The air steward arrived to whisper that one of the passengers did not love my aromatic potions wafting around the cabin. She told me that, personally speaking, she applauded me for turning the cabin into a temple of delight, but all the same she was obliged to pass on the message. I noted that the man who had complained was now snoring loudly with his mouth wide open. My aromatic potions had offered him sleep (I was convinced) but not myself. I was awake all night while ylang-ylang flowers hung about the boughs of his dreams.

All the same, I was very taken with ylang-ylang. Its sweet erotic fragrance was warm but harsh, like a hammer wrapped in fur.

It was on that long flight that I started to invent a female character who had a liking for ylang-ylang and could always be identified by this fragrance. She would be madly in love with a detached man whose narcissism she had to run away from, fast, if she wanted to do the things she had to do in the world. Like ylang-ylang, she would be sweet but slightly menacing.

The festival put their authors up in a skyscraper hotel, across the road from the Arabian Sea. The photographer asked us all to assemble for a photograph by the hotel pool and then he told us to do a thumbs-up gesture. I did not feel this was the right look for me. Its association with the popular gesture of male authoritarian leaders parading their erect white thumbs for the world's media was not something I wanted to imitate. My bare shins were being bitten by mosquitoes as the photographer snapped my lack of thumbs-up, and then, free at last, I dived into the swimming pool. There were crows everywhere, hopping and jumping and flying. High above the pool were two graceful whirling birds, their wingspan surprisingly wide in the sky. It was a pleasure to swim with the birds of Mumbai.

I met with Vayu Naidu, who was the convener of my talk at the festival. She wore a majestic pink and white striped sari. The elegance of the sari is unbeatable, the way it moves with the body, its flow and form. Vayu, in all her beauty, was now sixty years old, her silver hair cut short. She offered an astute critique of my books. In the questions afterwards, it was interesting to think out loud with the audience. I supposed that my literary purpose was to think freely, or rather for the books to speak freely on my behalf. If this sounds easy and obvious, it is not easy, not on the page or in life. Some people feel crazy when they try to deal with two contradictory thoughts at the same time, as if they fear they have done something wrong and need to purge the intruding thought before it muddies the water.

The point of thinking is that it will always muddy the water. So how do we live with our free thoughts and the mud?

In Western European realist fiction, what is a writer going to do (we wondered out loud) with the irrational, with synchronicities, with superstition and the private magic we invent to keep us out of harm's way, with the uncanny, with thought streams and digressions that contradict our attempt to fix the story? Can we accept that language is sacred and scared and it's scarred as well, because that's how we all are? I read to them a quote from Marguerite Duras:

> I think what I blame books for, in general, is that they are not free.
>
> One can see it in the writing: they are fabricated, organized, regulated; one could say they conform. A function of the revision that the writer often wants to impose on himself. At that moment, the writer becomes his own

cop. By being concerned with good form, in other words the most banal form. The clearest and most inoffensive. There are still dead generations that produce prim books. Even young people: charming books, without extension, without darkness. Without silence. In other words, without a true author.

Writing (1999)

We talked about how most literature, like life, is about how to have less and how to have more. Some people need to suffer less and some people need to suffer more. All the people we care about need to suffer less. Everyone is powerful when they feel heard and seen. It is a struggle to get anywhere near being heard and seen, so what does a writer do about that? If she invents stories in which her protagonists are seen and heard, does that feel true? The questions then steered towards my novel *Swimming Home*. We talked about the ways in which a powerful person can be vulnerable and a fragile person immensely powerful, and how a writer builds for her readers a trail of breadcrumbs in the forest. Perhaps another word for that trail is *story*, with all its interconnecting back stories, which might be another word for *histories*. We know the birds can swoop down any time and devour the trail but we are wired to want to find our way home. After all, to be lost without wanting to be found is to be in a place of deep sorrow. That is the place I had explored in *Swimming Home*. That is the place Virginia Woolf inhabited when she wrote her last letter to her husband before her suicide. The first word is very strong. It even has a comma, so she took a breath before she wrote her final words.

Dearest,

On the way to the book signing I met the writer Shreevatsa Nevatia, whose book *How to Travel Light: My Memories of Madness and Melancholia* describes his experience of depression and manic episodes. He told me that in one of his manic phases he had torn out the pages from his copy of *Mrs Dalloway* and scattered them across the streets of Delhi. He wanted everyone to read these particular pages because he identified with Woolf's character Septimus Warren Smith. Septimus is a soldier who has returned home from combat in the First World War. Shell-shocked and hallucinating after the blood and guts of battle, he is unable to pretend that his mind has not been smashed or that he can return to life as it was before the war. It is a tribute to Woolf that the words she had given Septimus were scattered by Shreevatsa over the pavements of Delhi. And it is a tribute to Shreevatsa too, his desire for everyone to understand those words. In every decade of my life, from twenty onwards, I have often thought about Woolf, witty, brilliant, despairing, filling her pockets with stones and walking into that river. I don't know why it is her suicide in particular that so personally hurts and haunts me. If I feel that her books speak calmly to me about the things that enraged her, I can nevertheless hear her rage, her breath, her chair creaking as she rearranges the position of her legs while she writes.

Meanwhile, the life of the festival (a life that Woolf might have enjoyed), an unreal and wonderful life, was happening all around me at a pace. Someone was passing me a plate of coconut jam biscuits. At the same time, I was also being introduced to an elderly woman who recommended a local tailor. She gave me his address and phone number because I had told her I had with me a dress I wanted copied. She asked me where I was going to buy the material for this dress? I explained I had brought with me a spare bed sheet of turmeric-coloured silk.

*

Vayu and I climbed into an auto rickshaw. This was the first time I saw something of Mumbai: the market stalls laid out on the pavements, piles of green beans, red pumpkins, aubergines, cauliflowers, ginger, turmeric, vendors talking into their mobile phones, their sandals placed neatly by their side. Somewhere else, an electric fan was balanced precariously on a wooden box on which a multitude of mirrored sunglasses were arranged, glinting like silver sardines. So much was going on, but we could not find Parmar the tailor. Vayu insisted that as he was lost to us, we were wired to find him. She rang him and he gave the auto driver directions. We eventually landed beside a small stall on a crowded street, and there he was, Parmar, his black hair threaded with silver. He unfolded my silk sheet and gave it a good looking over. It was a tense moment, as if he were searching for traces of bodily fluids, and sure enough, there was a stain. A small island of black ink.

That made me laugh a lot. It was from writing with my fountain pen in bed, but I began to think of language itself as having its own bodily secretions: blood, sperm, faeces, tears, urine, sweat, spit. In the old days the ink would have been octopus ink, a literal bodily fluid, or even soot mixed with water and binders, but now it was made from synthetic dye. When I finally croaked and was mummified in silk, clay and various aromatics, I would add sooty ink to the mix, perhaps on my eyelids.

Parmar didn't seem too worried about the ink on the silk. He measured me as I stood in the dry mud of the street and insisted I collect my dress on Monday at 2pm. I saw no sewing machine, just a pair of silver scissors, inlaid with gold handles. We then clambered back into our auto, the driver's bare feet sticking out of the door as he drove through the chaotic traffic. That is how I would like to drive too and in a way the auto reminded me of my electric bicycle, except with a wagon attached to the back.

Vayu and I went off in search of a chai masala by the sea. We were out of luck but the waiter brought us two cups of hot water and two Lipton's teabags. We talked about life and cooking and how turmeric turns everything an irrevocable yellow, including our fingernails and our clothing. And we talked about a line by the Bengali philosopher, poet and composer Rabindranath Tagore:

> It is very simple to be happy, but it is very difficult to be simple.

I confessed to Vayu that I understood how it was difficult to be simple, every writer knows that to be true, but I did not really believe his line about happiness. She said, 'Well, I'm happy to be sitting here beside you with a cup of hot water and a teabag.'

It occurred to me that I was happy, too.

Later, I walked out of my hotel and on to the seafront. It was there that I chose my bhel puri stall amongst all the other street-food stalls. I said yes to everything: yes to tamarind chutney, yes to chopped onion, coriander and tomato, yes to puffed rice and chillies and peanuts. I took my paper plate of this delicious snack and sat on a step near the makeshift shacks where many families lived. A sign was nailed to a wall: *No Washing of Clothes. No Cooking*. Everyone was cooking and washing clothes.

The sun was setting over the Arabian Sea, the ocean in which Gandhi's ashes were scattered in 1948, and from which turtles sometimes emerged to hatch their eggs, depending on the wild dogs that roamed the beaches. Sitting on that step, I watched a woman in a pink sari roll up a mat that had been laid out on the concrete floor of one of the shacks. An elderly man, perhaps her grandfather, had been sleeping on it. She was now cooking on a portable gas stove in the corner while he looked for his sandals. Crows began to gather near my feet as if they were my best friends. Their message was that it was only polite to share the bhel puri with them. An Italian film-maker at the festival, married to a man from Mumbai, had told me that when her mother came from Rome to visit her in Mumbai, she would throw chapattis to the crows from the balcony. Apparently, her mother thought this would bring her good luck. One day she saw the crows disembowelling a giant rat, their beaks buried deep into the bloody intestines. After that she went off the crows and never threw a chapatti to them for luck again. It was her hope to see four crows together because her neighbour had told her this meant she would become abundantly wealthy.

*

Two girls, maybe sisters, were dragging a bucket to a water pump. After a while they began to wash the piled-up plates in the bucket, talking to each other as excitably as the crows. An Indian woman at the festival had told me, 'If we educate girls we can change the world.' This is what I was thinking about while I finished my bhel puri, looking out at the Arabian Sea.

I returned from the slum shacks and warm sea breeze to the acres of polished marble floor and the chill of air conditioning at the hotel. All I had to do was cross a road to literally step from one world to another. I took note of that uncanny crossing and it obliquely influenced *The Man Who Saw Everything*.

At the festival in a room that used to be a Bollywood studio in the 1930s, I was offered my first glass of chai masala, fragrant with green cardamom, cinnamon, star anise and cloves. A writer from Kolkata came over to talk to me. He told me he now lived with his wife in their dream house in Goa. If I were to live there, he said, I would be able to afford a house with a cook and a driver. I could write my books and swim in the sea, rather than become decrepit in the English weather. He wrote down some places for me to explore in my quest for a house, but I really wanted to ask him how life would be for a woman to live there alone, a woman who was soon to be sixty. I did not ask this, because it seemed as if I was writing a future in which I was alone, without a companion. I was superstitious about writing that script, but the truth was that I believed it to be true.

There had been an intervention in this plot when a charming man from Delhi, who described himself as a tree whisperer, had whispered flirtatiously to me at a party given for all the authors. He told me that thirsty trees were a problem when water was scarce. Consequently, given the way the climate was changing, thirsty trees will become as extinct as tigers. All the same he loved the local fig trees best, what with their heart-shaped leaves. Did I know that figs always grow in pairs – aha, very wise of them, no one wants to be alone – and the juice from the bark is good for curing toothache? That is a good thing to know (his whispering lips were pressed close to my ear) should you become ill and there is no one to look after you. He liked his whisky and cigarettes and was amused that I smoked bidis. Why do you like them? he asked. I said they were aromatic. He explained that a bidi was tobacco wrapped in a golden temburni leaf. 'You must marry me,' he said. 'Yes, you must Come And Live With Me in the hills of Delhi, we can plant trees together and you can smoke bidis.' In the general noise and sociability of the party, where he was always by my side and what with the endless flow of vodka tonics with fresh lime, it seemed like a perfect life.

Yes, why don't you do it? Pack up and live in the hills of Delhi with the tree whisperer.

My house would be surrounded by sacred fig trees and he would whisper to the figs, encouraging them to start ripening in mid-April with a second flush in October. After all, he was elegant, fun and intelligent. I was about to phone my best male friend to tell him about the new plan, but then I saw the whisperer's eyes swerve towards a beautiful young woman who had just walked into the party in a sparkling minidress. I reckoned it was not such a good idea after all. All the same, I had been offered a new image of myself smoking bidis in the hills of Delhi. And something else. I tasted guava ice cream for the first time at that party. It was served with salt and chilli powder, a version of the sweet-and-sour craze that had taken off in the

UK with salted caramel. The guava ice cream was smooth, pulpy, fleshy, other-worldly. I vowed to learn to make it, if not in my new house in the hills of Delhi, then in my flat in the hills of North London.

A distinguished Swiss female architect at the party invited me to visit her house. When I arrived the next evening, I noted she lived alone with two fierce dogs and a fleet of servants. She showed me the stylish home that she had designed, beautiful objects and fabrics artfully placed in every room. Three curved white floor lamps reminded me of seagulls on Brighton beach. In truth, I preferred the real wailing gulls. As we stood by the fountain in her verdant courtyard, I wondered if I had been right to delete the fountain in the grounds of my grand old house and replace it with a river. I thought it was a good decision. It was as if this dead water was a banal imitation of alive water. Its repetitive burble was driving me mad, like listening to someone else's bad music. I longed to turn it off. Curiously, it seemed to me there was nowhere to daydream in her house, no nooks and crannies, no space that was not tamed. Perhaps it was a show house.

A table was laid by her staff and we ate dinner in awkward silence. I did not tell her about my dream of a grand old house with the pomegranate tree in the garden, or about the fireplace in the shape of an ostrich egg. It turned out that her cook had also made guava ice cream. I asked her for the recipe, which she kindly recited for me and which the architect translated from Marathi into English. I explained I was going to have a go at making this ice cream when I returned to the UK. My host seemed surprised that I did not have a personal cook. 'In that case,' she said, 'you must take back a few boxes of guavas with you. It is the season.'

She summoned her driver and waved goodbye while she stood by the dead fountain in the courtyard, her left hand gripping the collar of one of the fierce dogs.

Checking in online to confirm my flight back from Mumbai to the UK, I discovered the airline would not accept *MUMBAI* as my airport of departure. Mumbai was apparently an unknown location. India's largest city, at the forefront of the struggle for independence, did not exist. Did that mean the museum dedicated to Gandhi on Laburnum Road, the house built from stone and wood in which he stayed for over a decade, did not exist? And what about the two spinning wheels positioned near his mattress? Were they a delusion? I typed in *MUMBAI* about fifteen times but the airline would not accept it.

I walked away from my laptop and stared at the sky through the double-glazed windows that would not open. Meanwhile, the air conditioner made an Arctic climate in my room. If only I had brought a coat with me. I anxiously paced around the beige hotel carpet and then returned to my laptop. Peering at the screen, I realized I had in fact typed in *MOMBAI*. In South Africa, where I was born, a mum is a mom, and that is what I had always called my mother.

Mombai.

Mombye.

I could not accept her death.

My mother in Mumbai came back to me as a face in the sky. Her face was a cloud and I said, 'Hello Mom. Where are you? Where did you go?'

I did not know what I was crying about when I cried about my mother. Or was I crying *for* my mother? My momcry. What I remembered, as the years went by after her death, was not the whole woman but her expressions. Her eyes and mouth. The expression that was uniquely hers might be called *pondering*. Thinking about something. And then another question: why could I not see her whole body? I mean, see her standing up. She is always sitting down in my memories of her. And she did spend a lot of time sitting when she was old because she was lame and read books on her Kindle, day and night. All the same, I wondered if she always appeared to me sitting down or as a disembodied face because I had diminished her, made her smaller than she was, as if I could not contemplate seeing her stand tall, taller than myself.

I did diminish my mother. I wanted none of her problems. I wanted none of her suffering. I did not want to be like her. She offered me no vision of optimism for middle age or old age. Yet I loved her without measure. When I look back on this I can see that it wasn't really her job to offer optimism that she did not feel or possess. I think I held it against her because I needed encouragement, perhaps even a few comforting lies, *It's all going to be alright, you're going to be fine.* I don't think my mother could say anything she didn't mean. Really, she was not a missing female character, after all she was totally unique in her existential pessimism; she was just not the maternal female character I wanted her to be. What does *maternal* actually mean? If it implies comforting, protecting, teaching, nourishing, encouraging, lying, being the anchor in the storm of life, always being *there*, it is a tough call on any character to fulfil this roll call of qualities. Many women I knew who did not have children were much more skilled at all these impossible requirements.

*

My last evening in Mumbai was spent mourning my Mombai. When I called Vayu to thank her and to tell her how I had changed the name of India's capital city, she said, 'Not the first time it has been changed. And there is no reason why Bombay can't also be Mombay. By the way, cheer up, I know something very lucky is going to happen to you in the next three days.'

6

LONDON

I suffered the usual jet lag back in North London and woke up at 4am longing for the thin dhal I ate every morning in Mumbai for breakfast. I improvised a spicy sort of soup in my London kitchen: a tin of chickpeas, garlic, ginger, garam masala and then I pestled a withered root of turmeric and added it to the pan, in honour of my conversation with Vayu. Soon my London kitchen smelt of warming spices. I ate a small bowl of this soup while looking out at the dark sky. Memories of conversations in Mumbai came back to me. Two bankers who were urbane and sophisticated had told me they 'had a young woman helping with the house', age seventeen, whose mother had married off her older sister by taking a loan from a moneylender. This husband was violent and the sister needed to escape. So the bankers paid the loan for the mother and this meant that her second daughter, the bride's sister, had to work for them unpaid for however long it took to pay back the bankers for the loan. To be cleaning floors and toilets to free your female sibling from the blows of her husband was a new level of sisterhood.

I told my daughter about it when she woke up. She reckoned she would certainly do that for her own sister if it came to it. When her sister was safe she would run away, but was it possible to have porridge for breakfast instead of the spicy chickpea soup? And then she went into the bathroom and I heard her shout, 'Where are our hairbrushes?' Even though it was too early in the morning to be shouting, I noted that she had said *our hairbrushes*. It seemed to me that I had my own hairbrush, it was *mine*, and that she had her own hairbrush, it was *hers*, but in this moment, she had mislaid it. All the same, maybe because of the jet lag and maybe because of the Mombai incident, and maybe because she would be leaving for university in the late autumn, I was very touched by *our* hairbrushes and gave her mine as if it were hers.

She had been staying with her father while I was in India and it was tricky to keep all her stuff together between two homes.

While she took over the bathroom for an hour, I made her a pot of porridge. When her curly locks were primped and preened and she was sitting at the table, she dipped her finger into the chickpea soup and considered it gentle and warming on this winter's day. Yes, on balance, she was now in favour of a spicier start to the day and declined the porridge.

As she delicately spooned the soup past her glossed lips, legs folded beneath her on the chair, she thought it was a shame that I had not made parathas or rotis to go with this sort of dhal, which she thought would be very nourishing for her exam revision class. It was 8am. And then she asked me where I had put 'our door keys' and knocked over her glass of orange juice, soaking an important book I was waiting to read. I told her that should she ever be in the position to have to do domestic labour to free her sister from a bad situation, she would be sacked immediately. Scooping up her school bag, she pointed to the banana tree, as if it were somehow part of this conversation because it was my third child, or it might have meant something like *talk to the plant*, banged the front door and made her way down the grey and grimy Corridors of Love.

After she left I saw *her* door keys lying under the table. This reminded me of the key left on the tree in Central Park. Did my daughter think she could walk through walls to enter *our* flat or was she preparing to exit *my* flat and this was a gesture towards finally leaving home? I left the keys under the table, put the book on the radiator to dry out, and watered the banana plant, which was insatiably thirsty. Perhaps one day it might become as rare as a tiger. The next thing that happened on that jet-lagged morning was the post arrived. Amongst the bills was an envelope from America.

When I opened it (fingers stained with turmeric) I learned that I had been awarded a fellowship by Columbia University, to be based in Montparnasse, Paris. I was to be one of twelve inaugural fellows at the brand-new Institute for Ideas and Imagination. It would start just as my daughter was leaving for university in the autumn and I would be required to live in Paris for nine months.

What would become of the banana tree?

I stared again at the letter and then at my turmeric-stained fingers.

'Good morning Oracle Vayu,' I said to her in my mind, 'something very lucky has just happened to me.'

Still jet-lagged, my bag from India unpacked, and now without a hairbrush because my daughter had slipped mine into her school bag, I jumped on to my e-bike and cycled towards my old writing shed to tell Celia, my old shed landlady, the news. At the same time, I wondered what I was going to do about my new writing shed. I now rented two sheds, but it seemed that I would soon be a spectre in both of them.

Celia was my guardian angel but her wings could no longer lift her off the ground. She'd had a stroke in her eighties and was now unable to walk. Her spirits were very low as she adjusted to the new constraints of her life, but her blue eyes were fierce. Her little dog, Myvy, had just had her second eye removed by the vet. Celia had perfect sight but was glum. Myvy was blind but perky.

To change the mood, we decided that now and again Celia should read out loud to me a few pages from Leonora Carrington's novella *The Hearing Trumpet*. To listen to a woman the same age as the female protagonist in this novella, with many of the same problems, was a deeply moving experience. Carrington had given her elderly protagonists the dignity of imagination, humour, and some interesting thoughts about real estate.

> Houses are really bodies. We connect ourselves with walls, roofs, and objects just as we hang on to our livers, skeletons, flesh, and bloodstream. I am no beauty, no mirror

> is necessary to assure me of this absolute fact. Nevertheless I have a death grip on this haggard frame as if it were the limpid body of Venus herself.

The worst thing that old age had inflicted on Carrington's two elderly female characters was the painful surrender of their independence. They could not bear to be whispered about by those who now had control of their lives. Therefore, in Carrington's view, a hearing trumpet, in which the whispered words of one's adversaries could be heard clearly, would go some way to taking back this control.

> . . . think of the exhilarating power of listening to others talk when they think you cannot hear.

The story is a wild, surreal, joyful ride. Marian Leatherby (ninety-two years old) is given a hearing trumpet by her friend Carmella. Marian in turn has brought Carmella an egg, but alas she dropped it and can see that it's beyond repair. Carmella likes to smoke a black cigar. 'People under seventy and over seven are very unreliable if they are not cats. You can't be too careful . . .'

Meanwhile, back at Celia's ranch (the ranch was her terrible new reality) the two real household cats, Moony and Jan – 'She's the one who is soft,' Celia explained, meaning Jan had the softest fur – both slept on her feet at night, but Moony liked to change direction in the small hours and sleep on her chest. This worried the official carer, who thought the cat might inhibit Celia's breathing.

'Don't be fucking ridiculous,' Celia shouted, 'Jan, Moony and Myvy are the reason I don't kill myself.' In this sense, Celia was taking care of her precarious happiness, just as Carrington's novella had suggested she must do.

There is nobody that can make you happy,
you must take care of this matter yourself.

Celia Hewitt and her late husband, the poet Adrian Mitchell, had known me when I was first starting out as a writer, publishing poems and short stories in various journals and magazines. Every so often, Adrian would invite me to be the warm-up act at a few of his own phenomenal poetry readings. Now, all those years later, Celia asked me my age every day, as if she couldn't quite believe the answer. I told her again that I was fifty-nine, waving at the shores of sixty years. I wondered out loud if I could accept the walk to that part of the beach. Celia said I had no choice so it wasn't a matter of acceptance. She had decided to splash out on a new pair of spectacles to lift her spirts. The frames were made from fake tortoiseshell, as thick as her thumb. She told me that she had peered out of the frames as she was trying them on and thought, *Yes, I suppose that's what the tortoise does. It crawls out of its shell, peers at the world, shouts, 'Arise, ye wretched of the earth,' and crawls back inside.*

What most concerned Celia was that Myvy, being blind, could not climb on to her bed to join the cats at night. She did some research on her iPad and ordered a little wooden slide which could be attached to the bed frame. This meant the irascible hound could climb up on to the bed and sleep with her amongst the dreaming, soft cats. The image of this king-sized bed, the slide attached to it, three animals and a fierce old woman had no societal value at all, but it was of tremendous value to me. Perhaps I would propose Celia as a leading female character to the film executives next time we met.

Was she likeable?

*

Celia was one of the few women I knew who was very like herself. She was more like herself than I was like myself. She did not try to please anyone and certainly did not fit patriarchy's idea of what an old woman should be like: patient, self-sacrificing, servicing everyone's needs, pretending to be cheerful when she felt suicidal. If old women are supposed to not want to cause any trouble, Celia had decided to cause as much trouble as possible.

The trouble was how to live a creative life in old age.

The son of a friend of Celia's was living in the attic of her big house. In return for free accommodation, he was doing some of the caring along with the official carer. Sometimes it became too much for him, so with

Celia's permission he invited his best pal from Manchester to help out. These two young men, both of them students in their mid-twenties, kept the house cheerful, put up with Celia's volatile moods, cooked imaginative meals, played music that everyone enjoyed, and as anyone who has been in this caring situation will know, they had tremendous responsibilities to handle while they studied for their academic degrees.

Sometimes when I arrived to listen to Celia read from *The Hearing Trumpet*, one of the boys would be marinating a leg of lamb in something weird, like sultanas and balsamic vinegar, to which Celia, quoting from *The Hearing Trumpet*, remarked: 'I never eat meat as I think it is wrong to deprive animals of their life when they are so difficult to chew anyway.'

It seemed to me all over again that in every phase of living we do not have to conform to the way our life has been written for us, especially by those who are less imaginative than ourselves.

This is what *The Hearing Trumpet* is about too.

When Celia told me she had strange hallucinations about being somewhere that was not in her bed, I asked if the hallucinations lifted her to a place she liked to be? 'Oh yes,' she said, 'I am sometimes in the house in Yorkshire with Adrian – that was my favourite house. It had a fireplace and a river and a wood at the end of the garden.' I suggested she need not be scared of these hallucinations if her mind was taking her to a better place. She could agree to let herself enjoy the Yorkshire house, and, given she always dipped back into reality, that is to say, to shouting at the official carer for the sorrow of being stuck in a body that could no longer walk, there was nothing to worry about, except her tone with the official carer.

'Shut up,' she said.

'Not until I tell you my news.'

'Go on then.'

When I told her about the Paris fellowship, she pretended not to hear me, so I made my way through the garden to the old writing shed under the apple tree.

'Toto, we're home. Home!'

The Wizard of Oz (1939)

I had written three books in that dusty shed. Its tranquillity had given shelter to my writing at a time when my long marriage was shipwrecked and I was struggling to hold things together. I could see that I had been reluctant to separate from it when the house was put up for sale. My desktop computer was still there, sitting on Adrian's writing desk, now covered in a white sheet. Somehow I had believed it would be safe, my life's work inside the little black box that was an external drive called Time Machine, still plugged into the back of this giant computer. When my professional life had become a book-touring life, I'd had to get used to the tiny screen of a portable laptop. The large screen belonged to another sort of life, a smaller life, tethered to home. Also in the shed were many files stuffed with various drafts of my novels, as well as drafts of early plays that had been written on a turquoise Lettera 32 typewriter. I had loved that typewriter, also its matching carrying case, and wondered what had happened to it. The action of hammering its keys for the length of writing a novel would sometimes make a small callus on the tip of my second finger. In this sense, it really was a tool, like a scythe or saw; it required physical effort to use it. No way could it take me to the digital worlds of the Internet, but I enjoyed changing its ribbon and hearing the sound of the keys hitting the paper.

In one of the many dusty files stuffed with posters for various theatre shows and poetry performances, I discovered I had read a few of my poems with the anti-psychiatrist R. D. Laing at the Old Vic Theatre when I was eighteen. I had a vague memory of the man himself, but had admired his best-selling book, *The Divided Self: An Existential Study in Sanity and Madness*, written when he was just twenty-eight years old. Even then, when I was young, hedonistic and hopeful, I had known in some unspecific way that the ideas he was exploring about human consciousness, splitting, suffering and language were the lens through which the world made most sense to me.

> There is a great deal of pain in life, and perhaps the only pain that can be avoided is the pain that comes from trying to avoid pain.
>
> R. D. Laing, *The Divided Self* (1960)

My childhood in South Africa had been mostly preoccupied with trying to avoid pain. That was one of the things I did not want to know. Laing was right: it is such an effort. That's a good thing to know, but it's hard to know what to do with this knowledge. That's why I found my best male friend so relaxing. He basically had a passion for ignorance, which perhaps was a gift he had given himself and would one day dump in the bin. I said hello to him in my mind, and when he shouted back, 'Have you found a companion yet?', I realized I was missing him. What was I missing? His intelligence (which he kept a secret from himself) and easy company. We had both long ago agreed that no one is entirely stupid or entirely clever. When I texted him in Zurich to say I was back in the old shed, he texted back to say it was time I moved on and why was I not working in the new shed?

I hadn't yet told him about Paris.

Amongst the files I found photos of myself in my twenties. Should I dump them in the bin?

My daughters always complained they had no photographs of their mother when she was young. Perhaps I would save a few to give to them. It was all a bit overwhelming and after a while I couldn't wait to get out of there. By the time I walked back into the house, Celia and the unofficial carers and the official carer were all eating popcorn and watching a football match on television. Celia seemed quite involved in it. She did not want to read from Leonora Carrington today. 'By the way,' she said, 'if you're leaving for that fellowship thing in Paris, I don't have a full set of your own books.' I promised to bring them to the house next week. She scowled as if she couldn't care less and then added, 'Don't forget to sign them.'

I made an arrangement to come back before the house was sold to properly clear out the shed. 'Alright with me,' she said. 'Tell your daughter that if she's going to university in north-east England people are friendly there. She should learn some Geordie phrases. Your girl has always been a right bobby-dazzler.'

7

Rain fell quietly and gently on the trees in the car park of the crumbling block on the hill. As I helped my daughter pack her suitcases that autumn, I knew epic motherhood was now moving into a new phase. It seemed to involve many suitcases, both hers and my own, a journey to somewhere new, yet also a journey backwards to a life I had lived before having children.

I wondered if it was possible to be a matriarchal character who does not hold everyone hostage to her needs, ego, anxieties and moods. A powerful woman who is at the centre of a constellation of family and friends, yet does not conceal her own vulnerability, or mess with everyone else to get attention and empathy? I am not sure I have ever met her. I am certainly not her. How do we encourage, protect and nurture those in our care and let them be free? Perhaps the secret cost of true love is that it has to be free to fly away. And to return. Parents do not give children their freedom. They don't have to ask us for it. They will take it anyway, because they must. They are not our hostages, though I remember feeling there was some sort of mysterious ransom I was obliged to offer my mother in exchange for my freedom. Her children, if she loves them, are inside her, where they started life. It is a mystery to me to even write this sentence, never mind feel it to be true.

Yet in my unreal estate daydreams, my nest was not empty.

If anything the walls had expanded. My real estate had become bigger, there were many rooms, a breeze blew through every window, all the doors were open, the gate was unlatched. Outside in the unreal grounds, butterflies landed on bushes of purple lavender, my rowing boat was full of things people had left behind: a sandal, a hat, a book, a fishing net. I had recently added light green wooden shutters to the windows of the house. My best male friend suggested I add a septic tank, but saying goodbye to my youngest child was real enough for the time being.

I discovered that at fifty-nine I had a different relationship with my daughters, who were now young women of eighteen and twenty-four. Perhaps we could see that we were not that similar to each other, we were different, we did not have to be the same. This made us less judgemental, we could find enjoyment and inspiration in each other's company, and obviously we infuriated each other as well.

I learned a great deal from my children and their friends. Motherhood in the early years had been a long lesson in patience and submission to their needs. How could it not be like that? In later years, for some reason I had become a very good cook. I don't know how it happened, but when I separated from my husband and found myself mostly cooking for my daughters and their female friends, it was a pleasure to hear their oohs and aahs as various dishes were carried to the table, despite their pledges (secret and spoken) at various times in their adolescence to starve themselves into wraiths. Cooking for these young women wasn't my major playing card in life, they knew that. Some of them had started to read my books, and when they got to university they even wrote essays on those books. Yet I was never as happy as when I was cooking for a crowd of young women. It was an unexpected honour and I got a very primal enjoyment from their pleasure. They even joked that I should start a café called Girls & Women, and promised they would help out in the holidays.

'So what would you have on the menu for a starter?' I asked them. They reckoned the perfect entrée for Café Girls & Women would be Vodka & Cigarettes.

As usual, with the cooking, I was stepping into a role that I did not quite understand. It had been the same with motherhood in the early years. Perhaps it was even a political pleasure to nourish young women, who had such a hard time. Most of all I liked their appetite – yes, for the dish prepared, but for life itself. I wanted them to find strength for all they had to do in the world and for all the world would throw at them. As my majestic friend Agnes had suggested, I was furious about the pain that men inflict on women and girls. I mean, I had always been furious, but life had to go on, we could not be defeated by it. To be writer *and* chef-in-residence was an unwritten part for myself that I never expected to play. My respect for the valuable minds of these young women was immense. Sometimes their minds were fragile as well as powerful and that was alright with me.

Domestic space, if it is not societally inflicted on women, if it is not an affliction bestowed on us by patriarchy, can be a powerful space. To make it work for women and children is the challenge. In fact, is it *domestic* space, or is it just a space for living? And if it is a space for living, then no one's life has more value than another, no one can take up most of that space or spray their moods in every room or intimidate anyone else. It seems to me that domestic space is gendered and that a space for living is more fluid. Never again did I want to sit at a table with heterosexual couples and feel that women were borrowing the space. When that happens, it makes landlords of their male partners and the women are their tenants.

My daughter and I would depart from London at the same time. She would heave her giant suitcases on to the train, helped by her father and sister, and travel with them to a new city in north-east England. I would be heading on the Eurostar to Paris with a small dictionary of French phrases. It was odd, really, to discover I was so ignorant of the language in which all the books that had most influenced me were written. It was shamefully easy to forget that I had read them in translation, except for the names of roads, Rue La Fayette, Rue du Faubourg Poissonière, on the corner of which (I still remembered from teenage reading) was the bar in which André Breton's fictional lover, Nadja, would meet him, dressed in black and red.

As I could not rent out my flat because my daughters would need to return to it now and again, I asked Gabriella, a student who needed some extra cash, how she felt about bringing in the post and watering the plants. Especially my banana tree. We agreed a price and I handed over the keys.

My youngest daughter and I were nervous and excited about the start of our new lives. As Bachelard points out, a nest is a fragile structure that is nevertheless supposed to signify stability. We were going off to build new nests and my daughter had packed a toaster, a kettle, a frying pan and three new cushions to make her very first nest away from home. I cooked up a feast the night before we left for our new lives. There were many friends at the table, including Gabriella, and many more bottles of wine. Neither of us slept that well. I could hear my daughter whispering to friends on Skype at three in the morning and I was learning French from Juliette Gréco songs.

Je suis comme je suis.

Parlez-moi d'amour

The last thing I slipped into my daughter's hand was a brand-new hairbrush. She smiled and pointed with it to the banana tree.

'I hope Gabriella won't forget to water your third child.'

8

PARIS

> After all everybody, that is, everybody who writes is interested in living inside themselves in order to tell what is inside themselves. That is why writers have to have two countries, the one where they belong and the one in which they live really.
>
> Gertrude Stein, *Paris France* (1940)

A man was selling pink roses near Métro Abbesses for five euro. He looked hungry, down on his luck, so I bought a bunch from him. When I took the roses home to my new apartment in Montmartre, I discovered they were odd lengths; some were so short they did not even fit into a cup. He must have picked them in haste, perhaps in a park. He had wrapped them in a map of the Métro, the yellow line, C1 Pontoise, on the top left-hand corner. Some of the petals had come loose and stuck to the map. It looked like a poem. Maybe from Baudelaire's *Les Fleurs du mal.* I pierced a pin through the petals so they were attached to the map (Métro Rennes & Notre-Dame-des-Champs) and then stuck it on the wall with Blu Tack. Those Métro stops were not too far from the Luxembourg Gardens, where there is a rose garden.

> When you take a flower in your hand and really look at it, it's your world for the moment. I want to give that world to someone else.

The rose seller had given me some of his world. They were unhomely roses. These flowers did not freeze under the scrutiny of my gaze, they were breathing, very much alive, chaotic, displaced. They were roses travelling like people who have no homes across the Métro all night long, Nation, Pont Marie, Bastille, Mirabeau. At the same time, flowers were opening and closing, shivering, performing and growing on the stone walls of my unreal estate. And on the shelves of my new flat were my collection of Jean Genet novels, the writer who Jean-Paul Sartre had described as a burglar poet: *Our Lady of the Flowers*; *Miracle of the Rose*; *The Thief's Journal*, in which the toughest of men in prison were seen by Genet to be as fragile and sensual as flowers:

> There is a close relationship between flowers and convicts.

My new apartment was a five-minute walk from Sacré-Coeur. In a way it was a version of my apartment in London because it was located on a hill in a building that was once grand but unrestored. There were no grim Corridors of Love because the corridors were lovely, a circular wooden staircase curving its way up to the third floor. The bells of Sacré-Coeur were ringing while I unpacked my suitcases. A fir tree planted in the grounds cast a shadow over the front room. It was eating up the light. I wasn't sure that evergreen was a good idea. It would forever eat up the light. Perhaps on sunny days I could write under its boughs in the evershade, which meant I would have to buy a portable table that could fold up (like a flower) so I could carry it down the circular staircase. It had been hard to get my giant suitcases up this same staircase but the concierge had helped me. He was neither warm nor cold, tepid I think would be his mood, and that was okay with me. He told me that if I wanted to use the communal washing machines, he would give me a token in exchange for three euro and

I would need the code to get into the concrete bunker in the gardens where the two washing machines lived. So, he explained, if I wanted to wash my clothes, I must carry them across the garden into the laundry room and there was a special plastic rack in the flat for drying garments. I would also need a code to get into the main gate to the apartment. I quickly made up a rhyme to go with the code so that I would never be locked out late at night. It was quite a filthy rhyme and I was sorry not to be able to share it straight away with my daughters. Later, when I recited it to them, they never forgot it when they visited me.

The concierge went through the inventory of the things in the apartment for which I had paid a deposit: two cups, two knives, two forks, one cooking pot and a breadboard. There was a writing desk and one chair, two single beds in a bedroom that was smaller than the vast bathroom next to it. This bathroom did not have a bath, it had a tiny shower and big windows that opened up on to panoramic views of Paris. The inventory took a long time, considering there was not much to go over. The concierge sat on the one chair at the writing desk while I sat on the wooden floor because there was nowhere else to sit. He gazed at the empty walls (apart from my Métro map and rose petals), the biro poised in his hand, as if something momentous had been forgotten – perhaps a sofa, or a table and more than one chair? Downstairs, in the apartment below mine, I could hear the sound of an electric saw whirring. Ah, he said, yes, he had forgotten to include the plastic rack to dry laundry. At last we were done. When he left, I pushed the two single beds together, unpacked the turmeric silk sheets and duvet cover and pillow slips and began to make my nocturnal throne. I looked around the bare flat. So this is what an empty nest looked like.

Bleak. Or was it just uncluttered, light and spacious? Even in 1949, when she was writing *The Second Sex*, Simone de Beauvoir thought it essential that women emancipate themselves from a life tethered to home and children.

> The domestic labours that fell to her lot because they were reconcilable with the cares of maternity imprisoned her in repetition and immanence; they were repeated from day to day in an identical form, which was perpetuated almost without change from century to century; they produced nothing new.

All the same, I decided to disobey Beauvoir and find a local Monoprix to stock up on plates and cutlery. I was superstitious about a home that lacked the most basic implements to gather new friends around the table. When I made my way to Rue des Abbesses I was distracted by a shoe shop. In its window was a display of what used to be called 'character shoes', low heels, thin strap across the instep, maybe designed to resemble tap-dancing shoes. They were hard to find in London so I bought two pairs, one in black, the other in sage green. I made my way to the café opposite this shop, ordered a bowl of onion soup and a glass of red wine and sat on the terrace, watching people go by. All my homely thoughts about feathering the Paris apartment at the local Monoprix flew away. The concierge had told me it was located down the hill in Pigalle, which I knew was where André Breton, leader of the French surrealist movement, had lived. *Well, now you have some new character shoes, why not take a breather from making yet another home and step into another sort of character?* After all, I had never bought a pair of shoes in sage green before. Perhaps I was channelling Katherine Mansfield, who I could imagine wearing green shoes:

> Would you not like to try all sorts of lives – one is so very small – but that is the satisfaction of writing – one can impersonate so many people.
>
> *The Collected Letters of Katherine Mansfield* (1984–96), Vol. I

On balance I thought I was more like Apollinaire than Mansfield. He felt like a sort of brother because I loved him and laughed at him at the same time. He too had lived in Montmartre, as had Picasso, who joked that Apollinaire was the illegitimate son of the Pope. I took another peep at the character shoes lying in their box and felt slightly queasy. Could I step into a sage-green kind of female character? This particular colour reminded me of the house I had rented when I was twenty-six. One of the tenants made canoes for a living and he always painted the paddles this shade of sage green. At that time I was writing a play for the Royal

Shakespeare Company. The boiler room was the only warm room in the house, so it was there I had set up a desk to write. The canoe maker needed to dry the wet paint on his paddles in the warm boiler room, but the position of my desk made it impossible for him to do so. In the end we came up with a scheme in which he laid the unpainted poles over my ankles, while the paddles dried away from my feet. That was how I wrote my very first major commission. And while I was thinking about feet, I was reminded of how, when I was seventeen, I bought my first pair of shoes called brothel creepers from Shellys, also known as Teddy-boy shoes. Walking down the street in my very first pair made me feel like I was wearing a tattoo that marked me out for a meaningful life. Not quite winkle-pickers, their leopard-skin tongue (V-shaped) was surrounded by two inches of a thick black crêpe sole. To slip my naked foot into them was to literally walk on air. My brothel creepers were beauty and truth, genius personified, never mind they were rock and bop – that was not the point. They were my ticket out of suburbia, my exit sign from everything women were supposed to become. Their pointy toes tapped to the beat of rebellion; the shoes my father would never have worn, the shoes my mother would never have worn, in fact the shoes that not many girls wore but the ones that did were always gorgeous.

The character shoes had another vibe altogether. The downside was that I associated them with women who wanted to be a male artist's muse. The upside was they also resembled the shoes that dancers wore in the chorus lines of cabaret and vaudeville. These shoes were the opposite of trainers in that they were not cool at all. The trouble was that I loved them. Yes, I would slip my naked feet into these shoes and see what happened as their small heels clipped against the cobblestones on the streets of Paris. The same cobblestones under which lay the beach, according to the sixties graffiti of the student protesters. *Sous les pavés, la plage!*

The beach was a future that was not just capitalism. A new world lay underneath the old one. Now, nearly sixty years on from that slogan, the beach was strewn with plastic and trash, sewage and oil. I was reading the poetry of Paul Éluard in French to try and learn the language, and was quite taken by a quote attributed to him, though he might have lifted it from Rilke: 'There is another world, but it is inside this one.' If the ecology of the world was dying but there was another world inside it, perhaps I was going to leave my handprints on the walls of 7-Eleven, Carrefour and Intermarché to be studied by anthropologists in the other world.

*

Just to confuse things, while I was walking around Paris I was thinking about East Berlin in 1988, where I would set my novel *The Man Who Saw Everything*. Was communism the last big dream for the world? There would not be a beach in this book, but there would be a lake. A guard hidden in the trees would be watching two men swim naked, awkward with desire for each other. What did they dream for the world, these three men?

In the meanwhile I told myself: 'You have a flat full of things in London, why not have a flat full of nothing in Paris?' By the time I made it home, punching in the code to the main gate (which I rhymed with a few bawdy English words), I was happy to boil water in the only pot and to sip coffee from one of the two cups. I perched on the windowsill, looking out at the Gothic spire of Notre-Dame in the far distance.

*

I discovered that the whirring electric saw belonged to a woman living in the flat below mine. She was a sculptor in her twenties and she used the saw as the first tool to cut into marble, Perspex and stone. Then she used other tools to carve, poke and scratch these materials. Those tools made a banging sound, not a whirring sound. I glimpsed her working in the front room of her ground-floor flat. She had set up a table, dust on her visor, biceps popping in her thin brown arms. There were complaints about her electric saw still on the go late into the night, but I was mostly fine with it. Art doesn't keep predictable hours. If my laptop made a noise like her machine at two in the morning there would be complaints too.

When I glimpsed the insomniac artist with the electric saw in my local café, I noted that she was reading *India Song* by Marguerite Duras. The oddest line in this play is when a woman (Anne-Marie Stretter) says, 'For me . . . for some time . . . there's been a kind of pain . . . associated with music.'

Perhaps that's the way with music. What's the point if it doesn't hurt.

On my way to Montparnasse, which is where my fellowship was based, I would stop for a coffee near Métro Lamarck-Caulaincourt at a café called Au Rêve. Its broken blue-neon sign, *Au Rêve*, shone like a shooting star all day long. In my new character shoes I would walk at a pace down the cobblestones, past the bronze statue of the singer Dalida, around whom were usually a circle of tourists. Apparently, it was lucky to touch her breasts, so there was always a hand reaching out to stroke her nipple. One of her breasts shone extra brightly where the bronze had worn, like a revered religious relic. Sitting outside at Au Rêve, I continued to read the poetry of Paul Éluard in French. I was struggling with the language and would go over my own translations of some of his lines with disbelief, not at his poetry, but at my own fragile grip on the language . . . was it really 'the dark heart of my stare', were the windows 'deep' with shadows 'flowing'? It was a pleasure to have time to think about such things under the broken blue-neon dream at Au Rêve.

My new colleagues were thrilling intellectual company, challenging and convivial. They came from all over the globe (China, Malaysia, America, Kolkata, Nigeria, France), which meant the world of my fellowship was bigger than Paris. All the same, the City of Light was a seductive host, both modern and traditional. I was falling in love with her because she was confident enough not to smile all the time. If I was attracted to her, she was totally indifferent to me. One of my colleagues was renting a flat on Boulevard du Montparnasse, just behind Le Dôme. He said the apartment was situated above a boulangerie which started baking at three in the morning. Consequently he woke up in the small hours to the smell of bread rising in the ovens. It should have been a delight, but he said it was not as good as it sounds. Every morning he was suffocated by the smell of croissants and baguettes baking, it filled his nose, mouth, throat, and by 4am he was not waving but drowning in the sugar of various fillings for patisserie, in particular passion-fruit cream and the lemon cream for *tartes au citron* – which, my colleague told me, must be rough on the tongue but not *hostile*. Did I know the best lemons were from Menton? It was as if sleeping in a room above a boulangerie gave him special information. Eventually, he managed to drowse in sugar like a satiated wasp and catch up on lost sleep. Oddly, all this did not make him lose his taste for every cake

Paris could offer him. This particular fellow was twenty years younger than myself and excellent company. Of all the arts, the art of living is probably the most important, something at which he was especially skilled. I reckoned he could offer me a few tips as I reached my sixtieth.

This was on my mind when I made the pilgrimage to pay my respects to Simone de Beauvoir at her grave in Montparnasse Cemetery, where she was buried with Sartre. Even in death, they would be forever entwined. It was a very humble grave made from sandstone with multiple red lipsticked kisses pressed all over the stone. In this sense it was a grave of ghostly frantic kissing and I wondered if the impassioned lips were searching for Sartre or Beauvoir? I thought the lipstick kisses had not aged well in the weather, but maybe they were the right mood to celebrate the open relationship and companionship of two great French philosophers.

I was reading Beauvoir's *The Woman Destroyed*, first published by Gallimard in 1969, which meant she was around sixty when she was writing the first long story in this anthology, 'The Age of Discretion'. It is about a woman ageing, a long howl against the dying light of youth. The female narrator's husband/partner of many years begins an affair with a woman who the narrator feels to be intellectually beneath her own great mind. Her husband's hair is silver. They have both become quite inward when the story begins. Sexually, things are a bit stale between them, but they still find each other intellectually exciting. They are polite and affectionate with each other. 'I hope your work goes well,' he says to her, but her working day does not go well because she is raging at his infidelity.

'The Age of Discretion' is really a soap opera, maybe an existential soap opera, but with no fast cars or drunken street fighting. She is trying hard to remain a sovereign subject (Her Majesty, his queen) while he pursues his desires and tries to get a leg over.

Beauvoir is exploring her own feelings about Sartre's wandering, toady eye, and she is also exploring her argument that love is more destabilizing for women than it is for men. In her view, this is because a man's love of a woman is not what gives him his self-worth. I was no longer interested in exploring this kind of dynamic in my own writing. I could see no pleasure in it for the woman.

What came to mind while I was looking at Sartre and Beauvoir cohabiting under the kisses of their grave was Louisa May Alcott, writer, feminist, abolitionist. In her most famous novel, *Little Women*, the young writer Jo March marries her elderly immigrant German professor, but Alcott, like Beauvoir, did not marry. 'Liberty is a better husband than love to many of us,' she told her diary in 1868. I had always been interested in diaries. It seemed to me there is a shadow writer at work in a diary. Reaching for her truest thoughts, like a shadow she sees herself extended on the page, taller than her physical self. The diaries of Susan Sontag also show the experimental thoughts of a woman preparing to put her foot in the stirrups and get on to her high horse. At twenty-four she wrote, 'In marriage, I have suffered a certain loss of personality – at first the loss was pleasant, easy; now it aches and stirs up my general disposition to be malcontented with a new fierceness.'

The year Louisa May Alcott wrote *Little Women*, she lived alone in Boston. 'I am in my little room, spending busy, happy days, because I have quiet, freedom, work enough, and strength to do it,' she wrote on New Year's Day in 1868. When *Little Women* was published, she negotiated her royalties and held on to the copyright. Beauvoir, the heady intellectual existentialist, also read *Little Women* in her girlhood. Along with the rest of us, it seems that she too needed some encouragement.

It made me guffaw to think that before Beauvoir set off to study philosophy at the Sorbonne and to hang out with Maurice Merleau-Ponty and Claude Lévi-Strauss, she too had hooked up with the four American sisters Meg, Amy, Jo, Beth, and their pious, saccharine but spirited Marmee, who, it should be noted, was head of her household.

There are many resourceful and imaginative modern women who are heads of their households. Often described as 'single mothers', they experience the full weight of patriarchy's hostility to their holding dominant power in the family. His final last gasp at crushing her imagination and capabilities is to accuse her of causing his impotence. After all, if she can create another sort of household, she can create another sort of world order.

I would invite them all to enjoy the entrée (Vodka & Cigarettes) at Girls & Women, but only if my assistants could take a break from sitting on each other's laps while they plaited their hair and compared their new piercings. Together we would come up with a healthier entrée for Marmee, but you never know what a woman really wants because she's always being told what she wants.

At this time, I was also reading Elizabeth Hardwick's *Sleepless Nights*. She was a stunning writer, but I was worrying about the women she described as being left to 'wander about in their dreadful freedom like old oxen left behind, totally unprovided for'.

What was happening before dreadful freedom set in? And who are the old oxen left behind? Were they the women who are single or separated, bereaved, divorced? There was nothing in my life that had convinced me that freedom is dreadful. As Sartre suggested (he who was smothered graveside in kisses), we are also free to experience the consequence of our freedom. Boom! It was true that I was unprovided for, but then I never expected anyone else to put the baguettes on the table. The problem, it seemed to me, was that the female narrator in *Sleepless Nights* needed a man to give her kudos, or even to validate her existence. This was the same dynamic that rightly interested Beauvoir and which now bored me. It was a relief to swap the oxen for Georges Perec's rabbits. I was browsing (again) a few pages of Perec's *Species of Spaces*, admiring the way he put his low-key depression to work. Perec's book explores the everyday ways in which space is used and inhabited. Particularly interesting to me were his obsessive lists.

Attempt at an Inventory of the Liquid and Solid Foodstuffs Ingurgitated by Me in the Course of the Year Nineteen Hundred and Seventy-Four

. . . five rabbits, two rabbits en gibelotte, one rabbit with noodles, one rabbit à la crème, three rabbits à la moutarde, one rabbit chasseur, one rabbit à l'estragon, one rabbit à la tourangelle, three rabbits with plums.

He also had a taste for cheese:

Seventy-five cheeses, one ewe 's milk cheese, two Italian cheeses, one Auvergne cheese, one Boursin, two Brillat-Savarins, eleven Bries, one Cabécou, four goats' milk cheeses, two crottins, eight Camemberts, fifteen Cantals . . .

'This inventory,' writes Perec, 'offers the reader a somewhat oblique approach to my daily practice, a way of talking about my work, about my history and my preoccupations, an attempt to grasp something pertaining to my experience, not at the level of its remote reflections, but at the very point where it emerges.'

While I was new to Paris, I was keen to taste some of the cheeses he had scoffed. Dalí had apparently been inspired by the sight of soft and runny Camembert to paint his melting clocks in *The Persistence of Memory*. What kind of cheese was Brillat-Savarin? I discovered it was named after a lawyer and politician, Jean Anthelme Brillat-Savarin (1755–1826), who was also famous as a gastronome and had written an entertaining book, *The Physiology of Taste*.

> A dessert without cheese is a beauty with only one eye.

I thought he might be the right man for me, but then I discovered he fled the French Revolution in 1793, believed in capital punishment and promoted a diet that included no carbohydrates. The soft moist cheese named in his honour was made from triple cream. It had a natural bloomy snowy rind and was definitely a beauty with two eyes. And enormous breasts. Perhaps with a catapult in her apron pocket.

Life had taken a turn for the better. Imagination, Brillat-Savarins, ideas, the National Library, the Josephine Baker swimming pool, enough money, the companionship of fine minds, sublime jazz channels on the radio, reading the books of Annie Ernaux on the banks of the Seine, all of this was a big change from the years of keeping my family together in the crumbling apartment block on the hill.

My empty nest in Montmartre was really a version of my two writing sheds, except I could cook and sleep in it. I worked through the night on my new novel, while the sculptor downstairs worked through the night with her electric saw. When it became clearer to me that the main male character in *The Man Who Saw Everything* was going to live simultaneously in different points in time, I found that it was so technically hard to melt time in a work of literature, I had to write in all time zones.

> To work is to live without dying.
>
> Rilke

I was creating a male character who literally was trying to find a way of living without dying. He was running out of time. There were spectres, historical and personal, coming out to play in what remained of his life. He himself would become a spectre three seconds after the very last line in the book. There were spectres in the shadows of my own life too: childhood, Africa, love, loneliness, ageing, my mother, all the unreal estate in my property portfolio.

*

Meanwhile, I was learning how to negotiate the traffic across three lanes of Boulevard du Montparnasse and to dodge the electric scooters that were the fashion. People rode very fast on the pavements and slowly on the roads. I spent longer gazing at the spectacular shellfish on display at the fishmonger on the corner of Rue Lepic and Rue des Abbesses than I did at the art on the walls of the Louvre. A convivial man who had noticed me staring at the *crevettes royales*, *coquilles Saint-Jacques*, oysters, moules, razor clams and sea urchins said to me in English, 'They will undress for you tonight.' I quite liked the idea of a *coquille Saint-Jacques* undressing for me. 'I will dim the lights to give him courage,' I replied. The fish were laid out on mounds of crushed ice (as emeralds are displayed on satin cushions), glittering, abundant, bright-eyed. The godly *cabillaud* was cod, another sort of cod went under the moniker Julienne, and then the perverse twins, *lieu noir* (pollock) and *lieu jaune* (pollack). Rainbow trout was now renamed forever in my mind as *truite arc-en-ciel*. Three species of shellfish did undress for me that night. Or rather, I shamelessly undressed them. They erotically smelt of the sea. It was a *ménage à trois* because I made my first ever bouillabaisse for my colleagues. They ate this fish stew sitting on the floor because I did not yet have any chairs. I had invited the sculptor with the electric saw to join us.

It turned out that she was allergic to shellfish, but she made little human figures from bread, rolling the dough in her hands and then pinching and tweaking it. When these miniature sculptures were perfectly formed, she ate them.

When I finally got around to buying four chairs at a local shop, I again met the man who had predicted the shellfish would undress for me. He was buying a pepper grinder. 'You see,' he said, 'we must salute the chairs that have brought us together. Everyone is ringing the bells at the gate of the chateau to celebrate our rendezvous with fate.' He kindly offered to carry two of the chairs back home for me and we set off down the cobblestoned road, the chairs hooked over our arms. After a while he insisted we stop at a café for a pastis. I was carrying his pepper grinder.

It turned out that my rendezvous with fate was seventy years old. He wore a red scarf knotted around his neck and smoked his cigarette in a holder. When the pastis arrived, he told me about the friendly doctor to whom he had confessed he was no longer interested in sex. The doctor advised him to find someone who cares for him, but insisted that first he should find a woman to have sex with to get into practice for meeting 'the real deal'. So he took the doctor's counsel and that's exactly what he did. He had three rehearsals with a prostitute and then he found the real deal. His new partner, who he described as his *flamme*, was thirty years younger than himself.

So where was she now?

'She is at her tango class,' he said. 'The Argentine tango is her preference. It is more improvised than other forms of tango and it is danced in close embrace.'

He told me that while his *flamme* was pointing her toe at her dancing partner's spine, he would like to invite me to taste *babas au rhum*, also known as rum babas. Apparently, this fragrant sponge cake soaked in rum had made a comeback in French cuisine. We were sitting opposite each other on a terrace, the chairs I'd bought all piled up against a shop doorway. He leaned forward so that his nose almost touched my nose and began to whisper how he'd discovered that warm rum has the effect of Viagra on his body. Yes, he said, after a *baba au rhum* everything in the world could rise again, not just his penis, which he called his jaguar, but also Liberty and Equality, and birds with broken wings; even the soured friendship between Sartre and Camus might have lifted into sweet harmony had they only shared rum babas. When I declined the babas, he pointed at my sage-green character shoes.

'I commend them,' he said, waving his cigarette holder towards their toes. 'You look like the sort of woman who could be my second *flamme*.' We carried the chairs up the hill to my apartment and I insisted we leave them on the pavement outside the gate.

When I gave him back his pepper grinder, he looked at it mournfully and shuddered, as if it were a severed penis.

A few weeks later, when I bumped into him and his tango-dancing *flamme* in the interval at a concert, she told me that her boyfriend's jaguar was so erect after taking his rising potions (Viagra or *babas au rhum*?), he had to knock it against the fridge door to calm it down.

I never wore the sage-green character shoes again.

However, I did start thinking about how a jaguar can be many things: a car, an animal, a phallus. I made a note of this for *The Man Who Saw Everything* and wondered if a jaguar could also be a shape for fear. How about exploring the idea that every time a character called Luna was anxious, or thought she was being followed by the Stasi in communist East Berlin, she became convinced there were jaguars roaming the city? Why not try and grasp the weird ways in which the human mind can go anywhere? I was hospitable to this idea.

*

There were now four chairs around my table, six plates stacked on the shelf, six knives and forks in the kitchen drawer, eight wine glasses and a wooden salad bowl in the cupboard. In November my daughters came to visit me. It was the first time we had not seen each other for three months. We talked so animatedly on the Métro that we missed our stop. It was good to meet my daughters as adults who had things to do in the world. No one was in a bad mood. I gave them my bed and slept on a mattress on the floor of the living room. They did offer to take the mattress but they knew I liked to make coffee and write early in the morning. Yes, we were getting to know what we were all like.

I had bought three North African robes with hoods in a shop near Boulevard Barbès to wear as nightdresses. Two in pink, one in blue. My youngest daughter slipped the blue one on and started to sing a Taylor Swift song while her sister filmed her on her iPhone.

They asked me what present I would like for my sixtieth. I told them I was keen to make the guava ice cream I had tasted in Mumbai, so an ice-cream machine would be a piece of very exciting technology to me. When I had finally got the hang of it, we could discuss adding the guava ice cream to the menu for Girls & Women. They asked if I had a recipe? I took out a scrap of paper from the notebook I had kept in India and read it out loud to them. 'Yes,' I said, 'we will be peeling guavas and blending them to a pulp and we will eat this particular ice cream with chilli flakes and salt.' They stared at me in their hooded robes and my older daughter said, 'Don't forget that chocolate ice cream is really nice too.'

Paris was getting colder, the winter was coming in. Icy winds blew from the Seine. When my best male friend arrived, he was intrigued to see my empty nest. We had been friends for a long time and he knew this was my first experience of living without children in my home since I was thirty-four. I told him that my London flat was full of suitcases, mostly piled up in my older daughter's tiny symbolic room (she now lived away from home) and how it never failed to upset me to see it become a storage room. What with my youngest daughter travelling to and from university, and me travelling from Paris to London, it looked like a luggage shop. 'Well,' he said, 'I don't know whether you would wish it any other way?' I told him I yearned for a house and how I regarded the crumbling apartment block on the hill as a perch, but now I wanted to make another sort of home.

'But if you don't mind me saying this,' he said, 'why do you need a bigger place if it's just you living alone most of the time in the London flat?' It was hard to explain that my flat was full of stuff I'd collected over the years for the unreal estate in my property portfolio. Lamps, rugs, curtains, chairs, a copper fondue pot I had picked up in a flea market in Paris, bed linen, mirrors. There were at least three other homes inside my London home. When I asked him how Nadia, his wife, was doing, he just said, 'Oh, she is very Nadia-ish.' It seemed to him that she was still happy but pretending to be unhappy. This time I asked him why he thought she was pretending? He started to tell me but he was speaking with his hand across his mouth. I told him I couldn't hear a word, could he say whatever he was saying again. Apparently, she was pretending to be unhappy because she did not want to admit that he made her happy. Why was that? He thought that it gave him too much power. Nadia was keen to take some power back by pretending he was not the major reasons for her happiness. Here it was again, Beauvoir's theme in *The Woman Destroyed*. This time I had to confess I was interested, but I pretended not to be because it gave him too much power.

'It's hard for her to admit that she can only sleep when she is entwined with me,' he said, dipping his fingers into the bowl of stale peanuts on my writing desk. He started to choke and I thumped him hard on his back, three times. When he insisted on sleeping in the living room on the mattress, I told him I would prefer to give him my bed. 'You've got to be joking,' he said. 'No way would I let you sleep on the hard floor while I slept on your vast silken throne.'

The next morning he declared he had slept like an elf on a log.

We made our way to the Aligre market, stopping to look at a stall of African masks. The vendor begged me to buy at least two masks because he said he was cold and needed to get back to Africa. We laughed, but I did not ask him where in Africa, nor did I disclose that I was born in Africa too. The subject of where we are from is mostly not a two-second answer. It is a long conversation, maybe an endless conversation. I often left the African part of my biography out of conversation altogether because even five minutes wasn't going to do it.

My fellowship research was on the subject of the doppelgänger, so when I saw a mask that had two heads carved into it, that is to say, four identical eyes and two pairs of lips, I bought it. He explained that it was a dancing mask: the illusion was that the dancer's eyes were always on the audience. Then he showed me a mask with four eyes and two pair of lips and one nose, with a bird carved on top of its head. It was an incredible zoomorphic mask and I bought that too. I would feather my empty nest with these potent masks. I knew they embodied psychologies and rituals I did not yet culturally understand, but we would gaze at each other for a long time in my flat in Paris.

I had found another route into my thinking on the subject of the double, the doppelgänger. It seemed to me that in a time of rising nationalisms everywhere in Europe, in which difference was feared and demonized, it might be interesting to investigate the horror of similarity. What would it be like to meet our identical human double buying a pint of milk on a Sunday morning? My best male friend reckoned he would throw a punch at his identical self and knock him out cold if he met him in the Aligre market.

We made our way to Baron Rouge, where we ate oysters and knocked them back with wine from the barrel, quite rough wine. The oyster shucker had a machine to open the shells and he worked non-stop to feed the weekend crowd. After slurping his third glass of wine and ninth oyster, my best male friend shouted, '*Vive la France!*' I was embarrassed and pretended not to be with him, but he told everyone in perfect French that we had known each other since we were fourteen. Later, we walked through the market and bought fruit, a goat's cheese covered in ash, all the mushrooms that were in season and a bottle of Calvados.

All we really did together was eat and drink.

That night, in my empty nest, we made mushroom omelettes, followed by salad, cheese and fruit. The Calvados was light, golden and warming. We were happy in each other's company. He appeared to be mystified by his marriage to Nadia. 'She seems to disrespect me,' he said. I asked him why, in his view, should she respect him? He thought about this for a while, but seemed lost for words. This reminded me of the mother of one of my daughter's friends, when both our children were six years old. This mother had told me that my daughter seemed to have no respect for her husband. It just so happened that her husband was a very controlling man who was always snooping on his wife, and who could not separate himself from the enjoyment he gained from bullying his family. I was personally curious to know why she respected him, and in a way I think that was the question she was asking herself too. My best male friend was now waving his fingers at me. They were dusted with the ash on the rind of the cheese we had bought at the market. 'How about you? Found a companion yet? Or do you want to be alone as usual?'

'Well,' I replied, 'there's no point in telling me that being alone doesn't suit me. That's where I am.' I began to tell him about the woman who lived on the second floor. She was eighty and her male partner, or companion, lived upstairs. Sometimes he stayed the night with her and I would see him in the morning, going off to get the croissants.

'So why don't you make an arrangement like that?'

'Okay, I will set to it,' I replied, mostly to end the conversation.

'It's normal to have a partner,' he insisted. 'It's what normal people want.'

We both looked out of the window at the fullest moon, shining on the fir tree outside my window. Despite it being cold, we decided to carry two chairs down to the tree, holding on to our glasses of Calvados. We sat in the moonlight in our coats under the branches, listening to the scuffling of small invisible animals. It was the sort of thing we liked to do and it occurred to me that he was much cleverer than I was at getting the things he wanted from life.

The next day, as we stood in the queue on the Rue des Rosiers for the best falafels in the Marais, he said, 'I'm sorry I said that thing about normal people last night.' He grabbed my hand and kissed it gigolo style, but he was reading Tolstoy's *War and Peace* so he might have been imitating a nineteenth-century Russian aristocrat.

'Your stupidity has got you everywhere,' I replied to my best male friend.

A mutual acquaintance was waving at us. We waved back and Helena joined us in the queue. 'Hullo Helena,' he said, kissing her on both cheeks. 'We were just talking about what sort of life is a normal life. We're not after clarity, it's the tahini sauce we like.' My moronic best male friend had obviously morphed into Derrida for the day. He was wearing shades in the rain and carrying an umbrella with the name of a hotel written across it.

'And what sort of life is normal to live?' Helena asked, a bit mournfully. She was wearing a short, tight blue dress and trainers.

'I can tell you,' he said pointing to me. 'She wants a feral sea life. She wants to live in a swimming costume in the sun, always barefoot and barbecuing seabass. Correct?'

I nodded vaguely.

'It seems, Helena,' he said, 'what she wants most is to buy some real estate overlooking the sea and she is totally solo in that real estate. There are many rooms in her big house but all of them are empty. The beds are all made up but there is no one sleeping in them. She has a rowing boat tied to the jetty of her river and a pomegranate tree in the garden and bicycles in the barn. She swims alone, cycles alone, cooks, writes and sleeps alone. That's how she wants to live.'

'Of course she doesn't want to live like that,' Helena interrupted as if I were not there.

'Yes she does,' he said to Helena, draping his arm across my shoulder. 'When she is ninety she would like nothing more than to walk in the grounds of her real estate poking at snakes with her walking stick.'

Helena squeezed her almond-shaped brown eyes into slits. 'So can I ask, if I dare, you know, why did you two never get it together?'

We moved forward in the queue. To my relief I could see there were only five people in front of us. I was wearing my new black character shoes, but I had no idea how to be a nearly sixty-year-old female character.

'Well, that's a good question,' my best male friend said. 'She'd be up all night writing her books and she has always refused to have sex with me.'

Helena prodded my arm. 'Cat got your tongue?'

A busker started to sing a Romanian folk song to everyone waiting in the queue. It was quite a moody song and I was sorry to have to break from listening to it to join this conversation.

'Well, he is absolutely right in all he says,' I replied.

When we finally got to the front of the queue and bought three falafel pittas stuffed with salad and tahini sauce, we sat on a bench opposite a church and ate them there. The conversation turned to Helena. 'I don't like being alone at all,' she said. 'To live a life without physical intimacy is half a life.'

I thought that was true, but if that was the case the idea would be to live half a life very well.

'I need a lover to keep me warm this winter full stop,' she shouted to the pigeons.

'That's the right attitude,' my best male friend replied, obviously excited by the information that Helena needed a lover full stop. His blue eyes skimmed Helena's blue breasts, and then he punched me in the arm.

'Not like you, alone in the sun poking snakes with a stick while you smoke your pipe.'

I told him I'd prefer a cat to snakes but was happy with the pipe.

He started to laugh and then fumbled for his phone, which was ringing. It was a call from Nadia.

His voice was gentle and loving. He

listened to her speak for a while and then told her twice that he loved her.

I think he meant it. Really, I wanted him to mean it.

A close friend of mine from Berlin had said of her recently estranged husband: 'I do not trust that he ever had my best interests at heart. I do not believe he was interested in my well-being. I do not believe he could live warmly with me.' These were big sad things to not believe.

When the call ended, Helena turned to us both and whispered loudly, 'I want a man for January, February and the first week of March full stop.'

We wanted to know what was going on in the second week of March and the start of April. She told us that she could only bear so much adoring. Nine weeks would take her a long way. She asked my best male friend if he missed his wife when he was parted from her, like now, in Paris?

'No. I never miss Nadia. And I don't think she misses me either. It's so confronting when we are together, it takes me a long time to recover. But I adore her in all the seasons, January to December.' Helena wanted to know what he meant by confronting? He thought about this while he switched off his phone. 'I don't feel safe or comfortable when I am with her. Nadia scares me shitless, but if I lost her I would be inconsolable.' He and Helena started to talk at length about all this while I thought about my friend in Berlin and how it was her birthday soon. She would wake up alone for the first time in twenty years. While we sat on the bench I made the decision to visit her in Berlin and to be there for her birthday. We had known each other when we were both struggling to be artists and mothers in the turmoil of family life with our husbands and young children. We had spoken honestly to each other about this struggle. Somehow, attempting to do so in German and English had helped us to speak more freely. The language difficulties meant we had to find word choices that could be more easily understood by each other. The desire to comprehend what was going on in our very different circumstances was strong, powerful. As my Berlin friend had put it, searching for English words, she and I had *real human relations.* I knew she would not use those exact words in her own language, but I understood what she meant, though it sounded slightly official.

I learned a great deal from listening closely to her struggle for words. If she and I were both wounded, domesticated and humanized by our former marriages and children, we were definitely missing out on the adventure of Helena and my best male friend's current phase of human relations. She had slipped her leg between his legs and he was now stuffing his mouth with her uneaten falafel. Meanwhile, I was wondering from which airport in Paris should I fly to Berlin. Paris-Orly or Charles de Gaulle?

That night my best male friend did not return to the empty nest. Later, he told me he had spent the night with Helena full stop. It would seem that he was well on the way to losing Nadia and that he wanted to lose her and to be inconsolable full stop. While he gathered up his bag and umbrella and frantically searched his jacket pockets for his passport, he told me that Nadia had been seeing someone else for one month and six days, but he still loved her and so he figured that she would have it in her to still love him. I walked him to the gate, where the concierge was smoking a cigarette. When my friend opened up the umbrella with the name of a hotel written across it and made his way forlornly down the cobblestoned pavements towards the Métro, the concierge turned to me and said in English, 'But it is not raining.'

Helena called me late that evening. She had a lovely light-hearted way of speaking, as if seducing herself with her own words.

'Yes, of course we slept together. There was electricity in the air. Electricity is more exciting than a single naked flame. As for his wife . . .' Helena waited for an ambulance with full siren blaring to go by. 'All night he spoke to me about Nadia. Believe me, Nadia was raining all over us in the bedroom.'

9

I made my way just north of the Louvre to find a vintage fountain pen for my Berlin friend's birthday and then traipsed all the way to Le Bon Marché to find a bottle of ink called Carob of Cyprus.

On the way home I also bought her a box of the best *marrons glacés* and a soap in the shape of a cicada. That night, as the electric saw whirred in the flat below mine and a group of tourists sang 'We All Live in a Yellow Submarine' on the stairs of Sacré-Coeur, I spent a long time making her a card in my empty nest. The card was the Métro map in which the first peculiar roses I had bought for my new flat were wrapped, and to which I had now superglued the dried petals of these roses. I had added a new Métro stop to the map with a black felt tip and this stop was her name. Yes, she did not have a bridge or a plaque or a statue commissioned in her honour, she had a whole Métro stop named after her. What's more, the rose petals, just by chance, reminded me of the imagist poem 'In a Station of the Metro' by Ezra Pound.

I wrote Pound's words on the back of the map and dated the birthday card. It coincided with a miserable time in her life in which she was haunted every day by the apparition of the broken human relations of her marriage, but I knew that it would eventually lift. Meanwhile, I wrapped up the fountain pen and ink and *marrons* and the cicada soap separately in orange tissue paper, tied them with flamboyant orange ribbons, put all these presents in a carrier bag along with the Métro-map card, and started to pack my own bag for the journey. As I barely had a grip on the French language that had formed (in translation) all my youthful reading, I had to give myself time to navigate my way around Charles de Gaulle airport. So far, I could only speak a few lines from the Paul Éluard poems I was still translating – *the dark heart of my stare*, the windows *deep* with shadows *flowing* – but where is departure gate F26?

That night I slept badly and when I finally dozed off, my phone was ringing to tell me the cab was waiting outside. I had so little time to get to the airport that I did not bother to zip up my dress or tie the laces of my shoes. As I left the apartment, I picked up the garbage bag to dump in the big communal bins by the gate. It was cold and dark as I made my way through the grounds with my suitcase, the bag of my friend's birthday presents and the garbage bag. The taxi driver was good company. He told me his brother and father marched with the Gilets Jaunes every Saturday for economic justice. As far as he was concerned, Macron was president for the rich. Personally, he preferred Lady Gaga.

10

BERLIN

It was only when I going through Security at the airport that I realized I had thrown away the bag of birthday presents in the bins of my Paris apartment, along with the garbage bag. This meant that I arrived in Berlin, on a Sunday, empty-handed for my friend's birthday on the Monday. She lived opposite a medieval wall. Two industrial cranes hovered above it, reaching into the Berlin sky. This image of the past and the present existing simultaneously was something I was trying to grasp in the long writing hours for *The Man Who Saw Everything*. As Walter Benjamin had put it,

'The work of memory collapses time.' The past was a torment to my friend. She was trying her best to be cheerful, but there was nothing she could do to scare it away. She pointed to a tree growing by the ancient wall. It was a resting place for all the birds of Mitte. At around 5pm the sky was full of black birds with powdery jagged wings, flying towards its branches for the night.

All I could think about was the vintage fountain pen, the carob-coloured ink, the *marrons glacés* and cicada soap, and, above all, the Métro-map card. I said nothing to my friend about this for the time being.

Early that Monday morning, I made my way through a storm of icy December sleet to the department store Galeria Kaufhof in Alexanderplatz. It was closed. I would have to wait an hour before it opened. Things were getting worse by the minute. The sleet was now lashing down as I dodged queues of people in heavy coats waiting for trams under the tall concrete Television Tower, built in 1962 to display the might of communist power. Everything was grey, my fingers were numb, my coat was soaked. I found a fake-Spanish café in Alexanderplatz. The walls were covered in white tiles, and oddly, a shower tap poked through these tiles, as if it were once a bathroom. I sat on a straw chair under a big fake orange tree and waited for my cortado. In Paris I had bought seven large bottles of finest orange-flower liquid soap – Savon Liquide de Marseille Fleur d'Oranger (Corps et Mains) – for a bargain price at a pharmacy in Boulevard Raspail. Its scent was delicate and intense, a splash of summer in the winter months. I raised my hand and touched one of the plastic oranges. If I were to collapse time and place here in Alexanderplatz, the butterflies I had seen three years ago flitting through the citrus trees in the hills above Palma,

Majorca, would fly through the sleet and cranes and concrete of Alexanderplatz to settle on this plastic orange tree made in China. Memories of my twenties when I stayed in those same hills above Palma flew in with the shivering butterflies. It was a complete reset of my tastes, those early years in the Mediterranean. My boyfriend at the time would buy bread rolls, a tin of tuna, a tomato, a green pepper, and we would eat this humble lunch under the carob trees near the beach. Our desire for each other was immense, infinite; desire collapses time, too. I turned my gaze towards the old defunct shower poking through the white tiles. And then I looked away. The shower triggered an unfortunate collapse of time to Germany's Nazi history. Alas, this Spanish café was not conjuring a Mediterranean mood at all. Despite the jars of anchovies in the fridge, my association with the shower was the gassing of my relatives in Auschwitz. A phrase came to mind:

Let sleeping dogs lie. I wrote it down in my journal. It was a strange phrase, meaning leave things as they are, do not interfere and make trouble. As far as I was concerned, the sleeping dogs had their eyes wide open.

After a while I made my way across the icy, wet pavements to Galeria Kaufhof, just as it opened its doors. I had really made a mess of this birthday celebration. I bought flowers, smoked salmon, heavy pumpernickel bread, lemons and a bottle of champagne. Carrying my parcels out into the weather, a busker was singing, *I can see clearly now the rain has gone*. I thought he had a good sense of humour.

My Berlin friend was obviously awake by the time I returned.

'I thought you had run away,' she said. We opened the champagne while the industrial cranes began to move through the leaden sky.

She looked very beautiful and sad, so to make her even sadder I told her about the vintage fountain pen, carob ink, *marrons glacés*, cicada soap and the card. We both laughed at how her presents had ended up in the bin. My hair was still wet from the icy rain, which reminded me to describe to her my best male friend's last visit to Paris. We talked about the umbrella that had the name of a hotel written across it, and how the concierge didn't understand the internal weather inside my best male friend when he put up the umbrella. 'But it is not raining,' he had said, mystified. 'Nadia was raining on us all night,' Helena the seducer had astutely observed. My Berlin friend asked if I liked Helena?

'Well, I don't *dislike* her. She is lighthearted, reckless, vain. She is following her desire and desire is not always kind.'

My friend was trying to understand those words in English and figure how I could not *dislike* a woman who was chasing a married man. It was a little too close to the bones of her own situation.

'It is up to him if he wants to accept her invitation,' I said. 'It is his choice. He wants to suffer. He does not want happiness, but he always tells me it is Nadia who does not want happiness.'

My Berlin friend definitely thought Helena was not a likeable character and was starting to look baffled, like the film executives. She decided to change the subject.

'You must phone your concierge. Ask him to take the parcels out of the garbage.'

I did do this but he was certain the garbage had already been collected. 'If only you had told me earlier,' he shouted down the phone. It turned out that *marrons glacés* were his favourite bonbons, and had he known they were in the bins, he would have climbed in like a fox and devoured them for breakfast.

*

That night a birthday dinner was thrown for my friend in an old warehouse in East Berlin. Rainer was the chef. He was born in the south of Germany and his father, who was a carpenter, had taught his son the trade that his father had in turn taught him. I was surrounded by the tools of his new trade, which is to say that, as well as being a carpenter, Rainer had become a Japanese chef – so the tools of his trade were woks hanging from hooks, jars full of strange fungi, different kinds of miso, fermenting soybeans, pulses and barrels of sake, all of them labelled and dated. This warehouse had been restored by Rainer into a workshop and a space for living.

He had made a world of his own and it was a lovely world. A lush vertical garden grew on the concrete walls with all the intricate water pipes hidden behind it. He had built a mezzanine which was his bedroom. The futon that lay on its wooden floor was covered in geometric Japanese fabrics. In the centre of the studio stood a long, sturdy, monastic wooden table at which many friends had now gathered. While Rainer brought out plates of grilled mackerel, pickled cucumbers, miso, huge tempura prawns covered in panko crumbs and many other mysterious dishes, I spoke to an artist from Dresden. He had escaped from communist East Germany in 1985 and made it to the West. As a child he apparently fell into the river in Dresden. It was so polluted it took his mother a month to clean off the oil from his skin and hair. In some ways, he said, he believed he was still sick from that oil. He sometimes had nightmares in which he could taste it running down his throat. In fact, he could smell that oil in his hair on days he was feeling nervous. He had a tip for me: if you are making a fire and want to get damp kindling to take, coat it with vegetable oil and it will soon be crackling away. He seemed to have many stories that involved oil as the major theme. Perhaps oil was even the major character, which was alright with me.

Rainer was flushed from all the cooking and all the sake he had sipped while cooking. When he eventually sat down, he told me he had some real-estate dreams of his own. He wanted to buy a whole barn in rural Japan and bring it back to Berlin. He liked the geometry of one particular barn he had seen, but would not attempt to replicate its thatched roof. The barn would be taken apart in Japan and then re-assembled, plank by plank, in Germany. Yes, he would sleep every night in Japan and in Germany, all mixed together.

This morphing of place made me think of my childhood house in Johannesburg. We had lived in a low-slung bungalow in a road lined with jacaranda trees. Every day I woke up to an African sun in an African sky. I did not know, age nine, that the bone-white grass in our garden would be replaced by England's green and dewy grass. The jacaranda trees of Johannesburg and the daffodils of London were collaged inside me, all mixed together, as Rainer had put it. When I visited my elderly father in Cape Town, I would add something new to this collage: the mist from Table Mountain; great gasps of seaweed on city beaches near Seapoint; the icy sting of the Atlantic Ocean with its ghost ship (an oil tanker) always on the horizon, lit up at night like a fairy tale; seals turning in the waves; the tidal pools of Kalk Bay, where the Atlantic and Indian oceans merge, as Japan and Germany would merge in Rainer's new barn. Some of Gandhi's ashes had also been scattered in the Indian Ocean of South Africa, so he too travelled with the waves between India and Africa. These tidal pools were deep and salty with kelp and sea moss, the African sun (Hello my old friend) rising and setting over the mountain. In the collapsed time of memory, I was also diving into the brackish water of English ponds fed by springs from the River Fleet, serene and cold, fringed by gentle, swaying willow trees. These two weather systems and ecologies were morphed inside me, forever in conversation with each other. Rainer was still talking about the Japanese barn, once used for storing farming equipment. He would keep the old doors, pillars and beams when he put it up in Germany. He took out a pencil and drew a diagram, in which he explained the ceiling would be four metres high.

While I listened to his real-estate plans, I was thinking about a strange afternoon driving through Cape Town in an Uber with my daughters. The male driver was from Posada in Sardinia, but had come to South Africa with his parents in the apartheid years when he was a teenager. My daughters were sitting in the back seat; I was sitting in the front. We were passing roads that had now been named after some of the heroic men and women who had struggled to end apartheid.

As we passed Helen Joseph Street, I found myself telling the driver that when I was seven years old, I used to talk to Helen Joseph while standing outside the gate of her house. She was under house arrest, so she would be standing on the side of her gate that was in her garden. When I arrived after school, I would call for her cat, which was called Dinah, the name of Alice's cat in *Alice in Wonderland*. I didn't know if the creepy Cheshire Cat had a name. Sometimes I bought Helen a liquorice pipe from the sweet shop. While I chewed on mine, she would pretend to smoke hers. There were little red hundreds and thousands sprinkled on top of the pipe to give the illusion it was glowing. Helen was tall with silver hair and spectacles. Her accent (she was born in Midhurst, West Sussex) sounded very English to me. She looked like an unlikely freedom fighter, a white woman with silver hair who had trained as a social worker, became a trade unionist and fought all her life for human rights. A devout Christian, she had no children of her own but was stand-in mother to all the children, black and white, whose families were involved in the struggle to end apartheid, our parents imprisoned, or forced to live in exile. Helen Beatrice Joseph had been appalled at what she called 'the double oppression' of black South African women under the apartheid regime. She helped organize, along with Lilian Ngoyi, a march of 20,000 women to Pretoria on 9 August 1954, to protest against the pass laws that would curb the freedom of black women to travel freely in their own country. I did not know it then, but Helen was the first woman to be placed under house arrest for her activism; nor did I know that attempts were made on her life by the white supremacists of the apartheid regime. Explosives were sometimes pushed through the letterbox attached to the gate at which we spoke when I called for her after school.

The Uber driver was concentrating on the hazards of the chaotic road. I think he was a bit overwhelmed at my reminiscences, and so was I. When we passed Walter Sisulu Avenue, I said to him, yes, my mother and he were good friends. It was hard to know what to do with the severed parts of my own history on this drive down the roads of Cape Town. By the time we passed Nelson Mandela Boulevard, I could feel my daughters kicking me in the back.

I knew I sounded like a nutter. Perhaps I was the equivalent of a tourist in London muttering to a taxi driver as they passed a statue of Winston Churchill, 'Oh yes, my grandfather and Winston played marbles together when they were kids.' I could not put my South African past and my English present together in the way that Rainer could take down a barn in Japan and put it up in Berlin.

I had not dismantled my Johannesburg house and assembled it again in Britain. If I had once lived inside it as a child, it now lived inside me as an adult. The jacaranda trees lining the road were less ghostly. As a child I stood underneath their purple flowers waiting for the wind to blow the dry seed pods, which rattled like castanets in the breeze. It was true that memories of that afternoon in the Uber in Cape Town had tipped into the warehouse in Berlin and made time collapse. If I was made in Africa and England and Europe, the Uber driver was made in Italy and Africa, and Rainer was made in Germany but had run away to Japan.

Rainer was now tapping my shoulder in real time with his pencil. He had taken off his thick spectacles and asked if I would look after them for five minutes. He left the table and returned with a tray of Japanese custard eclairs. Everyone sang 'Happy Birthday' to my friend and we gave Rainer a round of applause for preparing the Japanese feast. When he returned to the table to retrieve his spectacles, I asked him why he had taken them off in the first place. He said he wanted to look 'super-handsome' when he received his round of applause.

My Berlin friend reminded me it was my sixtieth soon and asked if had made plans. When I confessed I had not thought about it yet, she told me her plan was to come to Paris and dump all my birthday presents in the garbage bins outside her apartment in Alexanderplatz. We embraced and she thanked me for making the journey to Berlin and Japan. I did not tell her that Africa and England had also come out to play.

11

PARIS

I had been struggling to speak German in Berlin and now as I searched for a taxi at Charles de Gaulle airport, I was struggling to speak French. The driver looked like a B-movie philosopher. He had wild white hair, a long white beard and was wearing a frayed tweed jacket. It was tempting to ask him a few basic philosophical questions: Is our universe real? What is the soul? Is doubt the origin of wisdom? As we made our way down the motorway and into the city, I began to recognize various neighbourhoods, but really I felt quite homesick for Britain. When my phone rang I saw it was Nadia calling from Zurich. She had a question for me. Could she stay in my London flat for a while? I told her of course, it was empty, and that Gabriella the pop-up concierge would give her a key. I liked it that Nadia did not explain why she wanted to stay and that it was a straightforward request. We both knew it was not straightforward at all. My phone rang again and it was my best male friend. 'I hear Nadia is going to stay in your London flat.'

I asked him why he was wrecking his life? He started to sob as the taxi crossed one of the thirty-two bridges in Paris. Neither he nor I ended the call, we just let it roll on while he cried. The taxi was now passing the endless sex shops of Pigalle, near where André Breton had lived and where Josephine Baker had opened her first nightclub. Somewhere close to Métro Blanche, Breton had offended the wife of Magritte (her name was Georgette) by demanding she take off the cross and chain she wore around her neck. I laid my mobile on my lap and looked out of the window at the Moulin Rouge on Boulevard de Clichy. The philosopher driver with his white hair and beard was asking me if I thought he was lost? Should he have turned right rather than carried straight on? His question was much more interesting than any of the questions I had been thinking of asking him. After a while my best male friend asked if I was still there. I told him I was still there. In this sense, he and I were attached to each other for better, for worse, for richer, for poorer, in sickness and in health.

Someone had parked a clapped-out vintage orange e-bike against the wall by the gate of my apartment. I stared at it for a long time. Where was the battery? Where were the gears? I was missing my e-bikes in London, my friends and the swimming ponds. I put the key into the ancient lock and opened the door of my empty nest. Death had come for my indoor plants. I liked the empty space in my apartment. It was like a bigger shed, but I decided my writing desk was in the wrong position. Before I had taken off my coat, I began to move it nearer the window. This involved removing everything from it, books, computer, printer, pens, a mug of coffee that had turned to slime. I dragged the desk to the other side of the room, found new sockets and plugged in adaptors, putting everything back except the mug of coffee. I went to the bathroom to wash the dust from my hands and stared into the mirror above the basin. What I saw in my eyes were my mother's eyes. I saw my mother staring back at me. What I mean is I could see her likeness in my face, in my expression, and for the first time in my life, this was not a bad thing. It was not something I dreaded. The loss of youthful beauty, for example. It was alright. It was okay. I was pleased to be connected to her. I felt my mother was with me in my flat in Paris, I really did feel that. She was looking around the apartment.

On the walls of the empty nest:

Two gold mirrors in the shape of eyes.

A rabbit mask and, underneath its chin, a brown egg (I had blown it four months ago and stuck it to the wall, in honour of the egg-shaped fireplace in Santa Fe).

Two African dancing masks with many eyes and lips (connected to my project on the doppelgänger).

A bunch of dried lavender from Provence (connected to my real-estate dreams).

A photograph of a painting of a garden bursting with abundant frothing yellow mimosa by Pierre Bonnard, titled *The Studio at Le Cannet, with Mimosa* (1938–46) (mimosa in full bloom being an atmosphere for a life I wanted).

A chalky-blue palmistry-guide poster showing the lines of the palm of a hand and its fingers (tip of the thumb is Will, length of the thumb is Thought).

A wrought-iron lamp with a yellow shade.

In the living room/studio:

A yellow velvet armchair.

A table with four chairs.

A writing desk and a chair.

On the mantelpiece of the fireplace:

A bottle of green chartreuse, made by Carthusian monks since 1737. Its herbs included: spearmint, fennel, thyme, angelica stems, sage, scented geranium, lemongrass, bay, lemon verbena, lemon balm, star anise, cloves, nutmeg, mace, cinnamon and saffron.

On the wall of the bedroom:

A black and white photograph taken by

Edmund Engelman of the road in which Freud lived with his family and had set up his practice: Berggasse 19, Vienna. The cobblestones on this road are wet, it has been raining, a man (we can only see his back) walks up the hill wearing a heavy coat and trilby hat, hunched into the weather. Perhaps he is a patient on his way to see Herr Professor Freud. The photo has a dark energy. In 1938, when this image was taken, the exterior of Freud's apartment was draped in a banner with *Juden* written across it. I had walked down this same road in Vienna to visit the Freud Museum. Engelman himself had written about the day he took this photograph:

> I remember that I was both excited and afraid as I walked through the empty streets toward Berggasse 19 that wet May morning in 1938. I carried a little valise filled with my cameras, tripod, lenses, and film and it seemed to become heavier and heavier with

every step. I was convinced that anyone who saw me would instantly know that I was on my way to the office of Dr Sigmund Freud – on a mission that would hardly have pleased the Nazis.

My mother was with me. I could feel her looking at this photograph. Her gaze was all over my empty nest. 'I want a house,' I said to her. 'I don't want a perch, I want a *major* house.'

Marguerite Duras had bought her major house, Neauphle-le-Château, in 1958, when she had sold her screenplays for a substantial sum. It was here that she wrote 'like a brute . . . ten hours a day'. The chapter titled 'House and Home' in her collected essays, or perhaps her collected thought streams, *Practicalities*, had stayed with me ever since I first read it.

Some women can never manage it – they can't handle their houses, they overload them, clutter them up, never create an opening towards the world outside. They can't help it, but they get it all wrong and make the house unbearable, so that the children run away as soon as they're fifteen, the same as we did. We ran away because the only adventure left to us was one all worked out by our mothers.

My mother had eventually run away from the adventure worked out for her by her own mother. This adventure involved learning shorthand and typing skills and then marriage at the age of twenty.

'Well done for running away.' It was something I had never said to her when she alive.

A while back, when I was staying with friends in the South of France, I had met a French woman in her seventies who had grown up in Saigon, Vietnam. On the off chance, I asked her if she knew Marguerite Duras, who had also lived her childhood years in Saigon. Yes, she replied, my mother was at school with

Marguerite. It was as if Duras had suddenly walked into the kitchen where we were eating couscous and drinking local wine. I wanted her to sit down and give me some tips on running my house and household, mostly because I was fascinated by what she described as the 'outer and inner order' in a house.

> The outer order is the visible running of the house, and the inner order is that of the ideas, emotional phases and endless feelings connected with the children.
>
> A house as my mother conceived it was in fact for us. I don't think she'd have done it for a man or a lover. It's an activity that has nothing to do with men. They can build houses, but they can't make homes.

My mother had done her best to run her household. As it happens, my father was better at making a homely home than my mother. All she cared about were her books. The colour of the curtains didn't matter to her as much as reading a novel that lifted her somewhere else. She was the least likely person to talk to about wanting a major house, but I could tell she was interested in my empty nest.

I was very blue for the weeks running up to my sixtieth. I suppose I was *triste*. I couldn't explain to myself why I was so low. When I wasn't researching and writing or sorting out my daughter's university accommodation, I trawled the flea markets and vintage shops collecting stuff for my unreal estate in the Mediterranean. So far, I had found a pair of wooden slatted blinds, two linen tablecloths, a copper frying pan, six small coffee cups and a watering can made from tin with a long spout. I was collecting things for a parallel life, or a life not yet lived, a life that was waiting to be made. In a way, these objects resembled the early drafts of a novel.

*

I was thinking about existence. And what it added up to. Had I done okay? Who was doing the judging? Had there been enough happy years, had there been enough love and loving? Were my own books, the ones I had written, good enough? What was the point of anything? Had I reached out enough to others? Was I really happy to live alone? Why was I so preoccupied with the phantasy of various unattainable houses and why was I still searching for a missing female character? If I could not find her in real life, why not invent her on the page? There she is, steering her high horse with flair, making sure she does not run over girls and women struggling to find a horse of their own. Does she scoop them up and ride the high horse with them? Do they scoop her up and take over the reins? Did that feel true? I hoped so. My fifties had been a time of change and turbulence, energetic and exciting. A time of self-respect and perhaps a sort of homecoming. So there you are! Where have you been all these years?

Winter had truly arrived in Paris. When I made my way to the exit from the Métro, a cold wind came in from the Seine and blew the hairpins out of my updo. I had to find sturdier pins. Or perhaps I should live with the curls and have my hair down for a while. There were days writing in my apartment when I realized something was wrong with my hands. They were so cold that my fingers had gone numb, even though the heating was on full. I could not get warm and worst of all my local swimming pool was closed down for repairs.

One of my colleagues knew I was melancholy. She took me out to dinner on the condition that I tasted something entirely new. We made a date and two days later we sat in a café on

Rue des Abbesses and I cracked into my first sea urchin. It was like eating the reproductive organs of an alien. Strangely enough, it was a poke of life and I even began to enjoy the harsh winter, its sharp nudge on my cheeks. My melancholy was lifting. I'm not sure it was all due to the urchin, but it was true that I felt most alive in the sea.

Something incredible happened. Another of my colleagues, Emeka Ogbu, was a visual artist and a DJ from Lagos. He thought it would be a good idea if, for my birthday, I invited some friends to dance to his music in the nightclub Silencio, for which he was going to soon be doing a gig. Silencio was a semi-private club for performers and artists, a place to meet and exchange ideas. Every room was designed by David Lynch, one of the film directors who had most inspired my approach to fiction. I took Emeka up on his offer and began to put together the guest list.

*

My daughters couldn't believe their mother was so cool as to be partying at Silencio. They arrived in Paris on the eve of my birthday and their gift to me was an ice-cream maker. A state-of-the-art ice-cream machine. I told them I would churn now for many years. When I heard that Helena had gone to Zurich to spend time with my best male friend, I decided to delete them both from my guest list and invite Nadia instead. All the same, he had heard whispers about the ice-cream machine and sent a friend to deliver a box of guavas via the concierge to my empty nest.

'Yes,' I said to my daughters, 'I am going to make us the exact same guava ice cream I tasted in India.' Every time I looked at them, I couldn't get over their beauty. When I told that to my daughters, the oldest said, 'Actually, I think guavas are quite ugly,' and I replied, 'No, not the guavas, I mean you.' They both agreed that all mothers think their children are beautiful, and gave me an update on the banana tree.

Perhaps I did not have one foot in Boulevard Death after all. Silencio had the perfect atmosphere for my sixtieth. Its design was mysterious, glamorous, a dimly lit inward world tucked into this world, and it was part of the history of cinema. There was even a smoking room, and this chamber in which one could *fume* was designed to resemble a forest of mirrors. There were nooks and crannies to have conversations and there was the adrenaline of the dance floor itself. Emeka's playlist drew us all in and then it sent us crazy. Every now and again I would look at him up on the stage, headphones over his ears, his arms in the air, our arms in the air. He gave us energy and conquered the room.

We all cooled off at 4am on the banks of the Seine. It was tempting to take off my sweat-drenched clothes and dive in, but Nadia told me, 'No, do not so much as dip your feet in the Seine, she has things to do. She is on her way to the English Channel, where she will flow into the sea at Le Havre.' I was not sure what she was going on about, except that perhaps she was talking about herself. Nadia was going to flow away from her husband. Yes, my best male friend was doing his best to lose his third wife, who was planning to free herself in Le Havre, or wherever.

It was slightly dizzying being a sixty-year-old female character. Perhaps a character is someone who is not quite herself. I think that is what is meant when someone in life is described as being 'a bit of a character'.

As the winter melted into spring, I found myself very homesick for my friends in England and Ireland. I was missing the trees and plants and flowers in my local parks and the dignity of speaking a language I understood. At the same time, as Brexit raged, I wondered what it would take to leave Britain and live elsewhere.

I re-read Milan Kundera's *The Book of Laughing and Forgetting* and began to understand the magnitude of his exile from Prague to Paris, the huge endeavour of learning another language, and actually *thinking* in that language when alone in the bath. Kundera had claimed his French identity. He described himself as a French-Czech novelist. It was a shock to realize all over again that I was part of the trail of writers who had made the long journey from their country of birth to somewhere else.

In February and March the flower shops were full of radiant yellow mimosa, feathery and fragrant. Its bitter-sweet, delicate scent made me swoon. Mimosa was a subtle, secretive, seductive flower and I started to add it to the trees in the grounds of my unreal estate. In fact my unreal garden was started to look identical to Pierre Bonnard's painting of his real garden in Le Cannet, in the South of France. This intrigued me because Pierre Bonnard's painting of abundant, sexual mimosa probably had many of Pierre Bonnard's desires and longing lurking in it. As I walked in my trainers (having ditched the character shoes) through the Luxembourg Gardens in spring, I wondered what I wanted that Pierre Bonnard wanted too. Parisians were sitting in green chairs that were positioned off the grass, which was forbidden to them, while glossy pigeons strutted freely across the grassy circle near the Orangerie. Maybe that's what Gertrude Stein meant when she wrote, 'Pigeons on the grass alas.'

When I walked out of the gate that opened on to the Rue de Médicis, I heard a woman call my name. At first I didn't recognize her.

Helena was waving to me, but I did not wave back because I wasn't sure it was her. As she sprinted towards me, I realized she had cut her brown hair short and dyed it blonde. Her new look reminded me of someone I knew, someone from the past, but I couldn't think who that woman might be. Nadia had long, jet-black hair, so maybe Helena wanted to signal her difference to her new lover's wife.

I felt awkward because I had not invited her to my birthday party. We each bought a cone of two different sorbets, passion fruit and rhubarb, raspberry and mango, and stood in silence with our melting cones, watching the traffic and tourists and cyclists. Eventually, I melted the silence too.

'Look, Helena,' I said, 'you don't want to become his fourth wife.'

She looked a bit sly and flushed. 'Well, how do you know what I want?'

I thought that was fair enough. When she smiled I noticed for the first time how pretty she was and how her new haircut made her look even more mischievous and sexy. I loved the way she used words.

'Y'know,' she said, 'sometimes you have to jump out of an aeroplane without a parachute. It's my choice. I want to be light. Free. I don't want to wear a helmet. I am my own commander.' She flicked her pink pointed tongue across her sorbet like a snake.

In 1969, Georges Perec had written a novel in which he left out the letter *e* for its entire length. The title was *A Void* in English and *La Disparition* ('The Disappearance') in French.

Without an *e*, Helena would be Hlna.

'I'm in love,' she said.

She was in lov.

She had jumpd into lov without a parachut.

Helena asked me if I wanted to see a movie with her that night.

She was without her lovr and was feeling lonly. I told her I was going to a talk by Gloria Steinem and asked if she wanted to come.

Helena said no, all feminists ate too much and so they had no energy for sex.

To like Helena was a hard call, but that didn't make her less amusing or interesting to me.

*

The talk was at the Mona Bismarck American Center. A long queue of women had formed outside, the Eiffel Tower to the right of us. Close up I could see the beauty of its geometric structure for the first time. When Steinem climbed on to the stage, the audience spontaneously stood up and applauded. Eighty-six years old, she still wore a thick belt with a large buckle that rested on her snaky hips. She took the applause in her stride, accepted it without false modesty, yet with no arrogance either. She had long ago told us the truth about the unpleasant aspect of truth:

> The truth will set you free, but first it will piss you off.

Steinem recalled how, back in the day, men would ask her if she attracted so much media attention because she was beautiful. She recalled a woman in the audience answering this question for her: 'We need someone who can play the game and win to stand up and say the game don't mean shit.'

My fellowship in Paris was coming to an end like my best male friend's marriage. Dismantling the empty nest in leafy Montmartre was a trigger to remembering all the other homes I had dismantled. My upper lip was trembling and so was my bottom lip, but it had to be done.

The concierge arrived to do the inventory so I could claim back my deposit. He sat down, waved his biro around and shouted, 'One pot, two knives, two forks, two spoons, two plates.' I was leaving three pots, six knives and forks, six plates, eight wine glasses, a kettle, four chairs, a yellow velvet armchair and two gold mirrors. He knew this, but he didn't care, he just needed the ticks on his inventory, and I needed them as well. We shook hands and wished each other well. That night I had a dream in which I bought a mansion in Paris and someone called Gregorio was living there too. I wrote it up for Sylvia Whitman, owner of the bookshop Shakespeare and Company, for a series of stories about living in Paris, which she was editing for *Port* magazine. I called it 'The 18th' because I was living in the 18th arrondissement.

12

The 18th

My former lover and I bought a mansion in Paris. A crumbling mansion. It had so many rooms that I had not yet had a chance to see all of them. Later, I discovered it had a swimming pool. Gregorio and his wife were there. One evening when I was wearing a backless silk dress, I knew he was watching my back while he prepared sea urchins for the feast. When I asked him if they were fresh, he said, 'It depends on what time of the day or night we eat them.' Gregorio was convinced he had bought these urchins on the Rue des Abbesses. It was true that my mansion might be located somewhere near there. We could hear the bells of Sacré-Coeur ringing.

Earlier we had watched tourists gather around a statue of Dalida, near Rue Girardon. Some of them reached out to touch her breasts because the guide said it was lucky to do so. I looked into Dalida's bronze eyes and she stared back. 'What a good time we're having?' she messaged to me, as I walked up the hill, towards my vast new property.

There were other people who had come to live in the house with us, mostly quite handsome literary men. One of them, I discovered later, was a Czech poet. In the morning he set off via the Rue des Trois-Frères to buy croissants. Yet when he arrived back at the mansion, he was sad to tell us the boulangerie was closed on Tuesdays. We had nothing to eat for breakfast and no milk for coffee. Gregorio volunteered to make his way to the Rôtisserie Dufrénoy to buy chicken and potatoes. I said I would come with him, but his wife pointed out that no one eats roast chicken and potatoes for breakfast.

It might have been spring because the flower shops in Rue Lepic were full of mimosa, yellow and powdery. A man was selling bunches of narcissus near Métro Abbesses, three for five euro. He must have picked them in haste, perhaps in a park. They were odd lengths and some were so short they did not fit into a vase. His brother was selling chestnuts. He roasted them in a tin which he had placed in a steel shopping trolley. When they were ready he wrapped them in a cone made from a map of the Métro, the yellow line, C1 Pontoise, on the top left-hand corner.

I went to fetch my friend Kiama from the Gare du Nord to show her my mansion. We detoured down Rue du Faubourg Saint-Denis to taste the bhel puri from the stall an Indian vendor had set up on the pavement, opposite a shop selling mobile phones. 'Everyone needs to call home,' he told us as he poured tamarind sauce over the bhel puri.

Kiama seemed disapproving of my mansion. 'I can't believe you have moved into this crumbling place just to be near Gregorio,' she said, 'and why is the front door to the house always open?' I gazed at the subdued but glowing pink plaster walls. The reception room was magnificent with its vast marble floor and many threadbare Persian rugs. When I looked up I saw an attic room with books on the shelves and wondered why I hadn't noticed it before.

Gregorio told me it was obviously a place that could be my study, and he quoted a line from Apollinaire: 'The rain so tender, the rain so gentle.'

When I finally discovered the swimming pool, I called out to Kiama to come and admire it. She wasn't that interested and asked me if the other people living in the mansion were paying rent? I said they were not. We both stepped into the pool. Kiama stood up to her waist in water. It was tense waiting for her to swim. She lingered on the edge looking out through the glass windows at the garden, which could be described as 'grounds'. Fleetingly, I noticed the fig trees needed watering. Kiama told me that the people living with us should pay rent, otherwise I would go bankrupt.

Later, I was walking with my former lover while all the people who were living in the mansion followed behind us. We were making our way towards the stairs that were near the Dalida statue, in the direction of Métro Lamarck-Caulaincourt. We were all very close and loving. I knew that this was a better way to live, to not be alone, to live in a large mansion with my affectionate former lover and other people – especially with the added erotic charge of Gregorio being there too.

I whispered to my former lover, 'Kiama says we must ask the others to pay rent otherwise we will go bankrupt.' I heard the people behind us, mostly quite handsome literary men, mumble, *yes, yes*, but not very convincingly. The Czech poet had threaded a sprig of mimosa through his buttonhole. Some of the literary men were touching Dalida's breasts. 'Return to your mansion,' she messaged to me, 'I used to have one near here too. If you see a black cat in your garden, it's mine.'

Kiama (watched by Dalida's bronze eyes) told me sternly that I should protect my grounds from poachers. Apparently, it would be a good thing to put in a gate with a code. All the apartments and houses in Paris had gates and doors that required codes to enter.

*

Kiama's words broke my dream. It was devastating to discover that I no longer owned a mansion. Its loss felt very raw. I lay awake trying to get back to my property, but no matter how hard I tried, I had no code to open the gate to my grounds that so badly needed watering.

After a while, I realized that all the literary men who were not paying rent were my former lover. Thank goodness that Gregorio had been watching my back. It wasn't lost on me that the mansion was crumbling, the fig trees were dying, the front door was always open, the Persian rugs were falling apart, but I was still happy, almost unbearably happy, that the mansion itself had been so grand. I was a dreamer who owned grounds and even a swimming pool. Above all, I wished that I had claimed the book-lined study.

I knew that some sort of change in my life was moving nearer to me after I dreamed about that mansion. The breeze from the Seine was doing odd things to my hair. It made it softer, wilder, tricky to pin up in a chignon. For the first time in a long while, I let my curls hang loose to my shoulders. There was so much to enjoy in Paris, but I still wanted to find that mansion in my dream. I looked forward to the swimming pool, to planting herbs and flowers in the grounds, to the unseen rooms and to lying on my back on the frayed Persian rugs, listening to the bells of Sacré-Coeur. The reception room felt like a life waiting to happen, somewhere between the present and the future. Yes, those unseen rooms were an exciting prospect. I was in mourning for two weeks after Kiama broke my dream.

Eventually, it occurred to me that Paris itself was the aphrodisiac and not Gregorio. I was happily living alone in the Paris of Apollinaire and the Gilets Jaunes. I kept coins in my pockets for the accordion players on the

Métro and had found my local boulangerie. It was not in the Rue des Trois-Frères. In the small park near my rented studio apartment, I glimpsed the hibiscus and daffodils poking through the French soil. They reminded me of home. When the shower did not work, I made my way to a hammam. The woman in charge gave me black soap made from olives and olive oil. I rubbed it over my body and sat in the steam, feeling less melancholy about the loss of my mansion. Later the woman massaged my feet with hot argan oil. When I returned home I noted the gate to my tiny apartment did indeed have a code. The last letter was *V* for *Validate*.

All the same, I was still furious with Kiama when we met in a café on the Rue des Abbesses on the day of the fierce hailstorm. We shared a bowl of *oeufs cocotte au Cantal* and sipped coffee as balls of ice bounced on the pavements. 'You demolished my mansion,' I said to Kiama, 'you bulldozed my property,' but she wasn't listening. It was Sunday and she was pleased to be with me in Montmartre, oohing and aahing over the *oeufs*.

13

LONDON

The first thing that happened on the night I returned to London was that I gatecrashed a literary party. I decided that if there was someone ticking off a guest list at the door, I would say I was Elena Ferrante. Or perhaps I would say that I was Lila, who had disappeared into obscurity but had briefly returned for crisps and cocktails in Bloomsbury, London. As it happened, the person at the door was a book-seller I knew well. She didn't even glance at the guest list.

'Are you back from Paris for good?'

I did not know how to answer that question.

'I hope so,' she said. 'By the way, avoid the wine and go for the gin cocktails.'

A male writer of some note, but not in my own hierarchy of note, had knocked back a few too many gin cocktails. This liberated his desire to find a female writer in the room to undermine. He thought that I would do and he cut straight to the chase without any small talk. 'Do you sometimes look in the mirror and think all this success came rather late in the day and so much exposure is rather vulgar, a total bore and awfully fatiguing?' He leaned back on his heels and waited for me to agree with him. His face was red and he was sweating. This was no way to greet Elena Ferrante just as she had walked into the party. She had exposure issues of her own and didn't want them thrown in her face before she'd even managed to grab herself a gin cocktail.

It was no way to greet poor, disappeared Lila either.

*

What was the question?

Do you sometimes look in the mirror and think all this success came rather late in the day and so much exposure is rather vulgar, a total bore and awfully fatiguing?

It was true that I had gained some mainstream recognition for my books when I was fifty, but as far as he was concerned, it shouldn't have happened at any age. What came to mind, given he was a Cambridge graduate back in the day, were the male undergraduates who had marched in the streets in 1897 to protest against the rights of female students to gain their academic degrees. These expensively educated men did everything they could to prevent women from outstripping them. They threw eggs and fireworks and even mutilated an effigy of a female student on a bicycle.

'Don't you think it's a total bore and rather vulgar and awfully fatiguing to achieve your academic degree?'

Yes, it had been a long haul to be acknowledged in a small way. I had started writing on a typewriter with a sheet of carbon paper between the pages when I was twenty-four. In my late teens I had read the dusty literary journals my mother kept stacked on her shelves, dating back to the sixties and seventies. I was interested in the interviews with brilliant male writers and barely noticed there was not a single interview with a female writer. Yet I had glimpsed a shape for my life when I was quite young. I knew I was a writer. Who is *she* then, this writer girl/woman? To not have been offended at the absence of women in the pages of those high-end journals was a terrible disconnect from whatever I must have felt at *her* absence. It was just normal. It was normal to be disappeared. It was normal to be discouraged.

Who is *she*? That is the question I was starting to ask in all my books. Not who am I, though that comes into it. How does *she* get along in a world that has voided her? For some reason I had never wavered from my own sense of literary purpose. In this sense I had taken myself seriously. Sometimes the phrase *she takes herself seriously* is seen as a flaw, as if taking herself seriously indicates she has aspirations beyond her reach, as if she should lighten up and have a good laugh at her own hopes. It has never ceased to fascinate me how there will always be a man and his female consorts who wish above all else to take down a woman who takes herself seriously. The women who want other women to have a good laugh at her talents and ambitions have usually fought very hard for male approval. They fear losing the respect of their male colleagues who need them to suppress other women on their behalf. If women are skilled at this brief, they never fail to look miserable.

It is, after all, filthy work.

So here I was back in England. The red-faced writer was actually blocking my way. It seemed he wasn't finished with me yet. The book that seemed to have drilled most deeply into his land was *The Cost of Living*. He asked me what he thought was a question about this book, but it wasn't a question. It was more like a reproach.

I had recently read from this book at an event in Freiburg, a city on the southern edge of Germany's Black Forest. It was haunted by its most famous son, the philosopher Martin Heidegger, who was rector of the university and a member of the Nazi Party. His student lover was the great political theorist Hannah Arendt. At the age of nineteen she had an affair with Heidegger, who was her tutor. He was thirty-six and considered this romance with his brilliant Jewish female student 'the most exciting, focused, and eventful' years of his life.

The audience, who mostly lived near this haunted Black Forest, had some questions to ask me. They wanted to know how I set about constructing a voice for the narrator, who is myself but not quite myself. I told them I reckoned the narrator had to do something that is tricky in life, never mind in a book. She must not make herself too big or too small. That is to say, she must not constantly undermine herself in order to beg readers to like her, nor must she make herself grander on the page than she actually is in life. It is hard to claim fragility and strength in equal measure, but that mix is what we all are. I explained how a quote from the artist Egon Schiele gave me a clue for how to proceed with the writing.

> In Vienna there are shadows. The city is black and everything is done by rote. I want to be alone. I want to go to the Bohemian Forest . . . I must see new things and investigate them. I want to taste dark water and see crackling trees and wild winds.

All writing is about seeing new things and investigating them. Sometimes it's about seeing new things in old things.

Another woman wanted to know, in her own words, 'how closely the book reflected my own life'. I told her the weight of living has been heavier in my life than it is in my books.

If this seems the wrong way round, it had to be that way. Otherwise I would have been defeated by my life. I did not wish to make light of the living, but rather to throw light on it, and shadow too, and then more light on the cost of living.

While the writer waved his soft white hands in my face, I thought, *Yes, Gloria Steinem is right, The truth will set us free and it will piss us off. Over and over again.* The truth was that he viewed every female writer as a sitting tenant on his land. And I thought about those clever young women, my daughter's friends, who had sat at my kitchen table in the crumbling apartment block on the hill. What I hoped for them was they would not get to sixty and have to endure being merrily mocked for their skills and talents.

If his class and education had taught him to regard his own thoughts as monumental, it had not taught him to read the work of women or writers of colour. Therefore he was bereft of some of the most important ideas for the world and the most exciting innovations with form. Yet his shameful ignorance had taken him a long way. In my reckoning, just one paragraph alone from the African American writer W. E. B. Du Bois was worth more than every book written by the red-faced writer.

> It is a peculiar sensation, this double-consciousness, this sense of always looking at one's self through the eyes of others, of measuring one's soul by the tape of a world that looks on in amused contempt and pity. One feels his two-ness, – an American, a Negro; two souls, two thoughts, two unreconciled strivings; two warring ideals in one dark body, whose dogged strength alone keeps it from being torn asunder.
>
> *The Souls of Black Folk* (1903)

Yes, in the present tense of this party, it was a peculiar sensation looking at myself through the eyes of the man blocking my way.

> And of course I am afraid, because the transformation of silence into language and action is an act of self-revelation, and that always seems fraught with danger.
>
> Audre Lorde, *Sister Outsider* (1984)

I pushed him out of the way and walked outside to join the crowd drinking bad wine. It was only later that I remembered he was the invited guest and I had gatecrashed the party.

14

GREECE

> Of all peoples, the Greeks have dreamt the dream of life best.
>
> Goethe

There were sixty-three stone steps to climb to get to my rented house. The doorway to this house was set in a stone arch covered in jasmine that was half alive in the August heat. It was a big, eccentric old house, built above the sea, a baronial Greek eighteenth-century villa that must have been quite grand back in the day. Now it was held together with stone, wood, donkey shit, piss and spit.

It was built on two floors and looked like a stage set for a Chekhov play. At the top of the house was a long wooden-floored attic room with high ceilings and a stone fireplace, an old waterlogged piano shoved in the corner. On its lid stood a brass telescope, a clock with fancy frozen hands pointing to four o'clock, and an ancient carved chessboard, all its players neatly arranged on the squares.

This attic reminded me of a barn; maybe it even resembled Rainer's Japanese barn, so I took a photograph and sent it to him. It had doors at either end of it, and these doors opened on to two wide terraces built from stone, one facing the sea, the other the mountains. Downstairs the large kitchen was cool and dark, with many baskets hanging from its wooden ceiling. I was told to put bread (and the local orange honey cake) in these baskets so the ants could not get at them.

Two ancient graters made from copper hung from a nail on the wall. They looked like weapons. Maybe Goddess Athena held one in each hand when she was born. As the myth goes, Athena was birthed from her father's head. It just so happened that Zeus, her father, had devoured her mother. Actually eaten her. Maybe in this kitchen. Their daughter, Athena, the girl child, springs from his head dressed in full armour, defended and ready for war. That was the patriarchal script written for Athena. It is a sad way to be born: armoured and ready for war. The living room was also built from stone, as were the three bedrooms with their high timbered ceilings, all of them cool and spacious, fraying kelim rugs on the tiled floors. The downstairs terrace was shaded by a tall pine tree, and underneath it stood a table and bench that had been hewn from stone. Twelve steps led down to a neglected garden. Grapes were still growing on the dying unwatered vines. Two olive trees were in better shape, as were all kinds of struggling plants I did not recognize.

Behind the house was a small farm. The roosters woke me every day, before the cicadas belted out their song from 7.30 in the morning, with an hour's break before resuming their call until 9pm. Apparently the singing cicadas are male. They are calling out to the females, who are mute. Therefore their endless song is of desire and they were so randy they drowned out any birdsong. If there were birds on a wire singing somewhere on the island of Hydra, as Leonard Cohen had told us, I could not hear them in August. Three blue-eyed dogs with wolfish grey fur lived on the balcony of the house next door. They howled every time someone walked up the sixty-three stone steps, which were always covered in donkey shit, also in the olives that fell from trees planted behind stone walls. At night I could hear the water taxis motoring across the sea.

*

In the third week of my long summer of living and writing in this house, I noticed a hole in the wall outside the bathroom. I poked my finger through it and sand started to pour out of the cracked plaster. Very fine sand. It went on and on pouring sand until there was a small beach by my feet. It resembled the rhythm of an egg timer, except with no time attached to it. After a while I wondered if the whole house would start to unravel and slowly bury me in the earth from which it was made in the first place.

In the end I turned my back on the relentless trickle of sand and went off to swim, picking two figs for my breakfast off the trees growing on the coastal path. The impermanence of the structure of this house stayed with me as I swam. Just as in the Borges story 'The Book of Sand', I wondered if the house, like that book, had no beginning or end. Would my laptop and passport be buried in sand by the time I returned? I half believed it could happen.

I did not so much *bury my head in the sand*, as the proverb has it for avoiding a situation or pretending it doesn't exist, as submerge it in the sea. While I swam I thought about ostriches, which are supposed to bury their heads in the sand but are in fact burying their eggs, turning them round in the earth with their beaks. The egg-shaped fireplace that I yearned for had once been a life form, a structure that held life within it, buried in sand or something similar. And what about ghost crabs, which burrow holes into sand to build their home? When the tides erase their home, they have to build another one. We are all tenants on the earth, which is our temporary home. Gazing at the shoal of miniature magical swordfish swimming under my feet, I realized I was frightened by the sand pouring out of that wall. Was it true, as Marx told us, that everything solid can melt into air? At least the muscular baby swordfish were beating their tails, zipping through the sea at a pace. It was a relief to see the house still standing by the time I had climbed up the sixty-three steps.

The nights were sweltering on the island. Couples walked hand in hand under the bright moon. Of course, I knew that Leonard Cohen had lived on Hydra for a while in his younger days and there was supposed to be an extra aura to the island because of him saying so long to Marianne. Returning from dinner with friends at two in the morning, I climbed up the steps to my house, past the cats sleeping on hot stone walls. It was as if the stones had as much breath, spirit and life as the cats, flint and fur lit by the stars.

I suddenly wanted to hear that song again. I had played it about a thousand times in my life, but that night I heard it as if for the first time. I suppose I had never listened to it at the age of sixty. I had first heard that famous goodbye when I was thirteen, when I wore frosted red eyeshadow to look like Bowie in his Ziggy Stardust phase. At that age, the idea was not to say goodbye to love, so much as hello. In the long stretch from thirteen to sixty, quite a few goodbyes had fallen from my lips. Where to start? Where to end? I could jump in anywhere with my own goodbyes. Goodbye to my husband of twenty-three years. That was terrible, inevitable, but given we shared children it could never be a final goodbye. We both agreed to live together, but separately, in our children's lives. Goodbye to my mother. I did not say the actual word *goodbye*. I did not want to frighten her, so I held her right foot in my hand and squeezed it. Goodbye, age twenty-four, to the first big love in my life. Maybe my first real love. His eyes. His lips. His thighs. His skin. Everything depended on how close his lips were pressed to mine. That goodbye was a break. A tear, a rip, a wound. The first harsh lesson that deeply felt love might not endure. All the goodbyes I had thrown like a bomb at those who were in love with me. Boom! There was one goodbye that I regretted above all others. Perhaps goodbye was not the right word and I should have said something else. Goodbye to my father when he returned from Britain to live in South Africa, after Nelson Mandela was released and the first democratic election was under way. Somehow my father taught me not to miss him. I don't know how that works, but in his old age at ninety-one years, I missed my father every day and told him that his only brief from me was to be immortal. He promised to do his best. I noticed he had become more emotional in old age and there was not one single WhatsApp message from him that was not signed off without loving words. My father is very skilled at knowing if fruit is ripe, so whenever I buy a melon or a mango I take a photograph of the fruit laid out in London grocery stores, send it to him in Africa and ask him which one I should choose. He studies the photo, and then in real time, fifteen seconds later, comes back: 'The melon on the left, second row.'

He is always right.

I cannot even imagine saying a final goodbye to my father. My mind shuts down any time I let myself think about it, so best to stick to mangos and melons for the time being.

And what about the wrenching goodbyes to friendships? Those friends who are very much alive, yet somehow the bond that held us together has fatally broken. In my experience that sort of break is to do with failing to move on with each other, or simply outgrowing the affection that once held us together.

Leonard and Marianne were now both dead. When Cohen himself was ill, he had written that great letter to her when she was dying – about how he suspected he would be following close behind her soon. If she stretched out her hand, he wrote, she would be able to touch his hand, he wished her a good journey and he loved her endlessly. Cohen in old age had made the long journey to that letter. It might be the very best thing he had ever written, addressed as it is to his mythic and personal past. The journey to that letter seemed to me to be the most important voyage to make at any time in life. He had not closed the door, he had left it ajar, and they would walk through it, separately but together, to their death. That night, in the deep heat of Greece, devoured by mosquitoes and reminiscences, I was thinking about all the doors I had closed in my life and what it would have taken to keep them ajar.

> If one were to give an account of all the doors one has closed and opened, of all the doors one would like to re-open, one would have to tell the story of one's entire life.
>
> Gaston Bachelard, *The Poetics of Space*

*

The next day I made Greek coffee in a briki, a little copper pot with a long handle, and hoicked down one of the hanging baskets from the kitchen ceiling. Inside the basket now lurked a slice of the famous orange honey cake. Not an ant in sight. The rasping cicadas were as manic as ever as I walked around the garden. The soil was dry and stony, unfamiliar to me, as were the half-dying plants and the insects that preyed upon them. I felt like a stranger in that garden. I had come from another sort of ecology altogether.

After a while I locked up the house and walked down the sixty-three stone steps to help a friend sort through photos of her late actor father. He had lived his last years on the island with his second wife. My friend and I picked grapes from the vines in the yard at the back of the house. Nine prickly pears lay soaking in a bucket of water in the yard. These too were a different ecology from the climbing roses and spring daffodils he had shared with my friend's mother, his first wife in England. I knew his head had been full of Shakespeare, yet his last walks on earth were amongst the goats and mules grazing on the dry golden hills above the sea.

Shall I compare thee to a summer's day?
Thou art more lovely and more temperate:
Rough winds do shake the darling buds of May

The darling buds of May had been replaced by other buds to be shaken by rough winds.

My friend was pleased to discover a photo of her father in 1954, dressed as one of a trio of dancing, singing sailors on a stage somewhere in England. As I told Nadia when she rang me later, 'Who doesn't want a dancing, singing father dressed in a sailor suit?' Nadia was devastated that her husband was romancing with Helena. Apparently she had only taken up with the new man to throw a stone at her husband's head.

'Listen, Nadia,' I told her, 'don't say goodbye unless you mean it,' and then explained that I had to rush to an urgent meeting.

The meeting was with a Greek film producer at a taverna in Vlychos, a twenty-minute walk on the coastal path from Kamini, which is where I was living. We sat at a table in the stifling heatwave and she ordered a bottle of ouzo and a bucket of ice. This was much more how I imagined meetings with film executives would be like. She even liked my shoes. A few years before I had flipped into a character-shoe persona in Paris, I had bought a pair of handmade brown canvas and leather brogues which were for sale in the window of a shoe-repair shop in East London. *They were something I had to have.* When I walked into the shop to make enquiries, they were exactly my size, the price reduced, apparently, from three hundred pounds to thirty-eight pounds.

The cobbler blew the dust off the box and then brushed the shoes with a small wire brush. The leather, the canvas, the whole atmosphere in their bespoke design was in conversation with everything I admired. They spoke of flâneuring and freedom and elegant nonchalance, they were neither male nor female and they were to be worn at all times, especially for courage at a meeting with a top-notch film producer. A box of cigarettes arrived at the table. Another bucket of ice – the last lot had melted. We did not talk about major and minor characters or whether these characters were likeable. We talked about our lives, our problems, the political atmosphere in our respective countries. A salad appeared on the table. A moussaka. A bowl of mashed fava beans. The film producer was impressive, tough, her long hair tumbling to her waist. I listened as she told me an anecdote about a situation that interested her. It interested me too. It was about a right-wing woman who was addicted to drink, drugs and orgies. The film producer wanted to trace how and why this woman eventually became a fascist. She suggested we give her a teenage daughter who does not agree with her mother's politics. I liked the way she had said *we*. The new ice was melting. I was slightly sunstroked by the time the sea taxi arrived to whizz her to the boat called the Flying Cat that would take her back to Athens.

My second meeting was with the sea. I dived from a rock into the big blue balm of the Aegean and saw no reason to ever leave it, no reason to ever say goodbye or so long. I wanted to swim in its embrace forever as the sun beat down on my shoulders. When I eventually agreed to part from it for a while, I saw that I could not put my bare foot down on the rocks to get a grip and lift myself out of the sea. There were spiky urchins clinging to every rock. It always amazes me that their cousins are the sea star. I called out to a young German man sitting on the rock and asked if he could throw me his rubber diving shoes. He could see my problem and happily did so. I slipped them on while treading water and this way managed to negotiate the spiky urchins. When I eventually lifted myself on to dry land, I put on my dress, laced up the brogues, started to make my way across the slippery rocks and immediately fell on my right elbow. The soles of these shoes were leather and the rocks were wet.

Later, when I gazed mournfully at the emerging bruises on my elbow and shoulder, I wondered what to do about these injuries. They needed some attention, but I was not used to needing this kind of attention and I didn't want to think about it. I roamed the port looking for a pharmacy and when I found one in a road behind the port, I stepped inside (wearing my brogues) and bought a strange oil infused with arnica. It smelt bitter and true. Part of my day was spent applying this oil to my elbow, finding diving shoes to dodge the urchins and another pair of shoes more suitable for climbing the many steps on Hydra. They were nothing compared to my brogues, but I had not realized my flâneuring shoes were made for the city and had the wrong sort of sole for a Greek island.

James Joyce had once quipped to an artist painting his portrait, 'Never mind about the soul, get the tie right.'

My tie was fine. I had to get the sole right.

I must take more care. More care of myself after decades of caring for others. I admit I found that hard. What did I find hard? Caring for myself. I had a few vague plans for the future but perhaps I would need to revisit them. In serious old age I would spend my days comatose in the sun with a plate of feta and watermelon. I would write film scripts and read and swim. And what about the bruises on my elbow? I had so far managed to live a reflective life and a physically active life. My days were full of people and of solitude. There is no such thing as not writing alone, but I could see that I had to make some plans. The only plan was my villa with its pomegranate tree, mimosa trees, its fireplace in the shape of an ostrich egg and the river and rowing boat called *Sister Rosetta*. I had no B plan, yet in life you need a few B's. I drank coffee in the port, holding the cup with my left hand because there were shooting pains darting through my bruised right hand.

A man was brushing the tail of his white mule, its saddle decorated with beads and ribbons. On extra-hot days umbrellas were put up to shade the donkeys waiting to carry tourist luggage up the hill. Two of the mules were lapping water from a steel trough. On balance, I preferred my electric bikes to carry my own burden. They did not have eyes.

*

My best male friend arrived on the island.

'Look,' I said, 'I don't want to know about you and Helena.'

We were sharing a plate of grilled octopus. It was an interesting taste but I no longer thought it was right to eat the world's most intelligent creature. My best male friend had a tentacle sticking out of his mouth. The octopus was so much more intelligent than him.

'Helena and I are just fooling around,' he said. 'Sometimes it's nice to do that. You should do more of that too.'

He started to tell me about a recent dream. I was quite involved with the pain in my shoulder. A cat climbed up beside me and placed its two paws on my left thigh. Its eyes were shut but I knew it could smell the octopus and was waiting to pounce.

'I thought that you of all people would be interested in my dream,' he sulked. 'Ever since you fell on that rock in your dandy brogues you've become mean and moody.'

I was thinking about the opening scene of the script for the Greek film producer. Its working title, 'A Woman, Her Lover, Her Husband and His Mother', preoccupied me. I was just about to ask my best male friend to tell me about his mother, when I realized I knew her. After all, he and I had been friends since we were fourteen. His mother had short blonde hair when he and I were young, a sort of pixie style that showed off her gamine features. She was a waif, more girlish than her son's female teenage friends, and she wore a very cool, shiny blue patent-leather belt around her tiny waist. How was it possible that my best male friend's new girlfriend had morphed into her lover's mother? The waiter brought us bowls of yogurt, topped with a kind of carrot jam that smelt like geraniums. This was definitely something I might add to the menu for Girls & Women. My best male friend was still talking about his dream. I was much more interested in the twinning of mother and lover, but I did tell him about a poem I was reading by Robert Desnos. As it happened, it was titled 'I Have Dreamed So Much of You'.

> I have dreamed so much of you that you are losing your reality.

The same could be said for my real-estate dreams. My unreal estate was losing its reality. As it wasn't real anyway, maybe that was a good thing. Actually, it didn't feel very good. Yet ever since that relentless trickle of sand had poured through the hole in the wall of the rented house, it was as if my real-estate dreams were slowly but surely also turning to sand. It hurt to let go of my grand old house with the pomegranate tree in the garden, but I was prepared to consider it possible that, like my rented house, I would not fall apart. A fly landed on the carrot jam. It became very still and dazed. Seduced and sedated by delicious, sweet, intoxicating poison, it seemed to have become paralysed by the sugar.

Perhaps my real-estate dreams were the sugar and I was the fly?

'You're drifting away from me,' my best male friend said. 'I can feel you drifting off to sea.' Actually, I was drifting back to dry land. The hole in the wall was a portal, not to another world, but to this one, in which I was endlessly searching for home, as if it were an elusive lover.

A few messages pinged on my phone. I took a look at them. My daughters confirmed the time they would be arriving the next day. The Greek film producer wanted to schedule another meeting, this time in Athens. Apparently, a window in my apartment in the crumbling block on the hill had blown open and the glass had cracked.

A small boat pulled into the harbour of

Kamini. The captain stepped out of the boat and handed a carrier bag to a young boy. It was filled with red snapper. Soon a wind would be up. The mistral, or *maistros*, was coming in. I would have to close all the shutters in the rented house.

'I'll tell you something to think about.' My best male friend reached for my bruised hand and affectionately squeezed it. I screamed. He continued anyway. 'Helena and I know how to share a day together. I am not sure you know how to share your day. You know, just pootling along with someone else. You just are not capable of it.'

The cat had polished off the octopus and the yogurt and the carrot jam. The conversation swerved back to Nadia. I noticed he spoke about her in the past tense.

'Nadia was lethally beautiful but totally inaccessible. That's what I found attractive but when I visited you in Paris I didn't find it attractive any more.'

'So you hooked up with Helena,' I piped up.

'Oh, so you're drifting back,' he said. 'What had been transmitted to me by Nadia is that I was not the sort of man she thought worthy of her. She never respected me. Oh my God, to be with Helena is such a relief. I'm exactly the man she thinks she should be with and why wouldn't that make me happy?'

I could see his point. He could slip from one woman to another like he slipped into his trousers every morning. I suggested that if his third marriage was on the rocks, he should be alone for a while.

He looked horrified. Why would he do that? There was no need for it. And while we were on the subject, why didn't I stop being alone for a while? That would be good for me, apparently. Again, I could see his point. 'By the way,' he said, 'let's have breakfast together tomorrow.' I had no idea why he was talking about breakfast while we were having dinner.

It seemed he did not want to be alone for one single hour.

I was thinking about Helena's words in Paris.

All night he spoke to me about Nadia. Believe me, Nadia was raining all over us in the bedroom.

Nadia was raining on him now, here in Greece, drenching him with her confronting love in the hot sunshine, and that made me think about cycling in the London rain past the statue of Peter Pan in Kensington Gardens. It had been raining on boy Peter, who could never grow up and accept the burden of adult responsibilities. The base of the statue was surrounded by tiny bronze mice, squirrels and fairies. Peter was blowing a trumpet or flute, locked in his boyhood forever. It suddenly occurred to me that my best male friend and I were the same age. Nadia, who was twelve years younger than him, had refused to take all the adult responsibilities off his shoulders. She was attracted to the adult man inside the boy and wanted him to stride into the world, not invincible, but capable, a man who could love a woman and did not require her to be an eternal girl. Yet his mother had been an eternal girl. He couldn't break the circuit. Helena was twenty-five years younger than him. She was happy to fly with her boyish codger for a while, no parachute, no helmet. She liked him just as he was, but he didn't like himself just as he was.

The cat was now making its way to his lap.

'By the way,' he said again, 'don't forget about our breakfast tomorrow.' He agreed with himself that we would meet at six the next morning. Yes, he would fly to the local shop to buy bread and eggs. He actually did say *fly*. It seemed that he had suddenly become an early riser, even an early flyer.

Next morning at around 5.30, I decided to go for a short swim before our early breakfast. I walked to my favourite rock and dived in. It was a peculiar sort of dive because of my bruised shoulder. The Aegean is the sea of the gods. It is ambrosia. Nectar. Warm but not too warm. It is friendly and it is luscious, like being held by a body that is not too clinging and not too detached. It washes from me the pain of thwarted hope for enduring love, connects me with my mother who taught me to swim, calms my fears about the future, takes the edge off the turbulence of my broken marriage, helps me reach for ideas yet empties my mind, brings me closer to both life and death. I don't know why, but it does.

The short swim had turned into a long swim, maybe a mile or so around the tiny pebble coves. I lay on a rock to get my breath back, looking out at the olive trees and then up to the sky and over the hills to where the mules and donkeys grazed on the golden grass growing around sun-bleached stones. A flock of tiny birds flew from an invisible nest to another nest, just above the fig trees hanging over the coastal paths. Did that mean they had moved home or were they just visiting friends?

My hair was drying in the early morning sunshine, my feet were brown, my skin smooth, my body satiated by sea, salt and sunshine. I realized that I was not sharing the day with my friend. Maybe it was true that I did not know how to share my day. I looked for my phone. There were six messages on the screen and it was now 8.30. Two of them were from my daughters. The other four were from my best male friend, who had left on the early boat for the island of Poros, where he was meeting Helena. That is why he had wanted breakfast at six.

I laughed on that rock for a long time. Perhaps he had tucked a flute into his pocket and the small animals of Poros would gather around his feet as he disembarked from the boat, his third wedding ring glinting in the sunshine as he waved to his new young lover.

> You have to be very fond of men. Very, very fond. You have to be very fond of them to love them. Otherwise they're simply unbearable.
>
> Marguerite Duras, *Practicalities* (1987)

I was very fond of my best male friend full stop.

I made my way to the port and enjoyed breakfast with the big rusty industrial barges which carry goods to the island: washing machines, watermelons, bags of flour, bottles of water. The waiter had a tattoo inked near his ear. He said the letters spelled *Peitho*, the name of his girlfriend. I bought twelve oranges at the grocery store and walked home. Back at the house, which felt like the shadow house I had yearned for all my life, I watered the neglected grapevines and the half-alive honeysuckle bush, while the cicadas, forever desiring, sang in the tall, ancient pine tree. I swept the terrace and hosed it down, and while I was at it, I hosed myself down with the soft rainwater from the well.

None of this real estate belonged to me, but I felt I belonged to it.

I wrote every day in its long, timbered attic and finally acknowledged I did not have a tranquil relationship with language because I am in love with it. I asked myself, what sort of love? Language is a building site. It is always in the process of being constructed and repaired. It can fall apart and be made again.

I was happy cohabiting with my rented house. As I hosed down the stone table and bench on the terrace, I was sorry, very sorry, that owning it was beyond my reach. It felt like a blow, a humiliation, as if I had somehow failed to make a story go my way and end it with a long-held dream come true. I would have to accept that I just didn't know how to bend the story in my favour. I would not have to call an electrician to mend the air-conditioning fans on the ceilings or a plasterer to fill the hole in the wall. It would have been like repairing part of myself to do so.

Yet my encounter with this rented house was a taunt, a provocation; it made me feel more alive. If I was full of desire for its ambience and grace, the fact that I did not have the means to buy it only accelerated my desire. Perhaps it was not the house but desire itself that made me feel more alive.

> Maybe it is a good thing for us to keep a few dreams of a house that we shall live in later, always later, so much later, in fact, that we shall not have time to achieve it.
>
> Gaston Bachelard, *The Poetics of Space*

In the distance I could hear the clanking of a bell. A mule was walking up the hill. It carried a fridge on its back in the heat of the late afternoon. It made me think about the wooden horses standing on the windowsill of the crumbling apartment block on the hill in North London. They looked similar to the ancient horses that were once painted on the walls of caves. The glum corridors felt far away. I was not sure I wanted to return to them. It wasn't that I wanted to make a phantasy life on this island either, not at all, but for the first time since I unmade the family home, I felt I did not have to be punished by walking through those corridors every day.

I walked into the kitchen and found the oranges I had bought at the port. Was there a gadget in the cupboards to squeeze their juice? I rummaged around and found it hiding under a colander. It was an effort to squeeze twelve oranges on this primitive plastic object. I poured the juice into a jug, threw in a handful of ice cubes and put the jug in the fridge. I felt excited as I made my way back to the port to wait for the boat, the Flying Cat, that would bring my daughters to the island. They would have to climb sixty-three steps to get to this temporary, loving house.

It was a balmy early autumn evening at the port. The church bells were ringing. The big news in town was that the bakery had added a sweet cheese pie to its pastry selection. Donkeys and mules stood tethered to each other by the boats, waiting for their next burden. As I mingled with the crowd, I wondered if I considered myself to be an unwritten sixty-year-old female character waiting for her daughters to arrive on the Flying Cat?

Or did I consider myself to be a sixty-year-old female character who was continually rewriting the script from start to finish?

I was both those women.

So then, now that I was a sixty-year-old

female character, both unwritten and constantly rewriting the script, what did I value, own, discard and bequeath?

Give me a break, I said to myself at the port. It's enough to work long hours to pay the bills and rent a house in the sun and to not steer your high horse off the cliff on a Tuesday.

That is enough.

The ship pulled into the shelter of the harbour. Two men ran to catch the ropes that would tether it to the island. The Flying Cat opened its doors and a whoosh of petrol blew into the warm night. I waved to my daughters (no wedding ring on my finger), all three of us smiling and shouting hellos as they struggled with their luggage down the ramp. When I invited them to sip cold orange juice in the garden of our rented house, they told me they would prefer a cold beer. But what about the twelve oranges I had spent an hour juicing on that old plastic device, scooping out the pips and pith? They did not want to be told what it is they want full stop.

We found a port-side bar and joined the men with silver beards playing backgammon, rolling the dice, flicking their worry beads. A crowd of teenagers sat at a table nearby, braiding each other's hair. The boy who had taken delivery of the bag full of red snapper was now eating gyros with his father. As my daughters sipped their beer, which was called Mythos, and gave me an update on the banana tree I had bought in Shoreditch High Street, I found myself still searching for the answers to my questions.

I supposed that what I most value are real human relations and imagination. It is possible we cannot have one without the other. It took me a long time to discard the desire to please those who do not have my best interests at heart and who cannot live warmly with me. I own the books that I have written and bequeath the royalties to my daughters. In this sense, my books are my real estate. They are not private property. There are no fierce dogs or security guards at the gate and there are no signs forbidding anyone to dive, splash, kiss, fail, feel fury or fear or be tender or tearful, to fall in love with the wrong person, go mad, become famous or play on the grass.